CRUMB QUILTS

SCRAP QUILTING THE ZERO WASTE WAY

EMILY BAILEY

DAVID & CHARLES

www.davidandcharles.com

CONTENTS

INTRODUCTION

Quilters are thrifty, resourceful and creative. Crumb quilts appeal to all of these qualities. They are the ideal way to use up all your lovely scraps and express your artistic nature through beautiful quilts – and they are economical to make, too.

Canny quilters realize that, yard for yard, tiny scraps are just as valuable as the larger pieces in their stashes. Throwing them away would be a shame. But crumb quilts allow the imaginative quilter to find ingenious ways to use even the tiniest leftovers which otherwise might be wasted. Sewing them together to form one-of-a-kind fabrics, which are cleverly incorporated into your projects, produces gorgeous original quilts full of interest and memories. And using fabrics you have already purchased is totally guilt-free, leaving you with extra pennies to spend on more fabric and other quilting goodies.

Gaining inspiration from the past, both from previous generations of quilt-makers and fabrics left over from your own earlier projects, crumb quilting is a great way to create truly personal designs. A perfect remix of your previous makes, crumb quilts showcase your particular style, colour preferences and eye for beauty.

So embrace the crumb quilting method and use your super-powers to bring joy, beauty and comfort into a world in need of them all.

TOOLS AND MATERIALS

Cutting tools

A lot of your success in quilt-making will come from precision in cutting. Having the right tools makes accuracy much easier.

Cutting mats

I like to use a 24 x 36in self-healing cutting mat for cutting out my background and crumb fabric pieces. I prefer a 12in square self-healing cutting mat when making crumb fabric, as the smaller size means I can keep the mat next to my sewing machine so I can trim off uneven edges as I go.

Quilting rulers

Gridded acrylic rulers for quilting come in many sizes. Use a 6 x 24in ruler for cutting pieces for your quilts. When making crumb fabric I like to use a smaller ruler – a 4 x 8in ruler is my favourite as it is small enough to use next to my sewing machine but long enough to allow me to make a good-sized chunk of crumb fabric.

I have found that a flying geese ruler really cuts down on waste when cutting up my crumb fabric. Squares, half-square triangles and quarter-square triangles can all be cut from a strip of fabric. (Cutting instructions for using a flying geese ruler are given in the projects where I have found this ruler most useful.)

Rotary cutters

Choose a rotary cutter that fits comfortably in your hand. Using a sharp blade will save time, making cutting easier and more accurate (uncut threads or untrimmed sections can cause crumb fabric to distort your work). If you need to go over the fabric more than once to cut it, it's time for a new blade. Trust me, taking time to replace a blade is well worth it.

Scissors

It is useful to keep a small pair of scissors or snippers near your sewing machine for cutting threads and tidying up bulk around the edges of your crumb fabric as you make it. A seam ripper is also handy, as when things don't go together as planned a little unpicking may be in order.

Sewing tools

The right tools make things easier and help with accuracy. The following will help you be successful in creating your quilts.

Sewing machine

Your sewing machine does not need to be fancy. As long as you can sew a straight ¼in seam then you are good to go. Zigzag and other decorative stitches are a bonus, but not necessary. If you wish to free-motion quilt, you will need a machine that allows you to drop the feed dogs.

Presser feet

I recommend using a ¼in presser foot to help with accuracy when piecing. But a strip of masking (painter's) tape lined up ¼in from your needle will also work. I like to use an open presser foot when doing appliqué as it gives me a better view of where I'm stitching as I sew around motifs. A walking foot is necessary for straight-line quilting and a darning foot is required for free-motion quilting. Personally, as I like my quilting to be more organic, I don't use a walking foot, finding a darning foot to be sufficient.

Machine needles

Universal needles in size 80/12 or size 75/11 work well for piecing and quilting. With sewing machine needles, the larger the number the thicker the shaft. If you are experiencing broken needles, try using a larger needle. It's a good idea to change your needle after 6–8 hours of sewing as they do get blunt, and change immediately if you nick a pin, or your needle bends or breaks. Skipped stitches and puckering can occur when your needle is dull, bent or the wrong size.

Pins and clips

Long straight pins, with a ball or flat head, that are sharp and designed for quilting are useful when matching up seams and points. As well as evenly applying borders and longer sections in your quilts, dividing up long seams and pinning them will help to eliminate wavy, ruffling edges.

Safety pins are my favourite tool for basting quilt layers together. Use the large curved pins designed for quilting, not standard safety pins. The curve makes it easier to get the pin down through the quilt layers and then back up to the quilt front. You will need at least one hundred pins to baste a quilt.

Binding clips are perfect for holding your binding in place while sewing it on. A less expensive option is little girls' hairclips, which you can often find in discount stores. You can also buy quilters' clips in a range of sizes – the smaller ones can be used in place of pins for some jobs.

Pressing

A standard iron and ironing board are ideal for quilt-making. When making crumb fabric, use steam and spray starch to get a clean finish and make cutting later easier. Remember to press and not iron. Pressing is putting the iron down and holding it. Ironing is moving the iron around, which can distort your fabric.

Marking tools

From time to time you will need to mark on your quilt tops, such as marking a quilting pattern. Water-soluble markers are a good choice, as is tailor's chalk. Choose what will show up best on your fabric and will be easy to remove later. I sometimes use a Hera marker – a plastic tool that creates sharp light creases – which I find particularly useful for marking out straight guidelines for quilting.

Design wall

A design wall is a great asset when it comes to arranging your crumb quilts. Essentially, it is a giant flannel board where you can lay out your quilt. Quilt blocks and fabric pieces stick to it without pins, allowing you to step back and get the big picture on how your colour and design elements are coming together, so you can get a feel for what your quilt will look like before sewing it together. While it doesn't always eliminate 'kissing cousins' (two of the same fabric touching), it does help. You can use a flannel-backed tablecloth pinned to the wall or make your own 'wall' from foam-core board and flannel.

Appliqué tools

The right tools to turn will help you to achieve perfect appliqué motifs.

Interfacing and fusible web

Lightweight fusible interfacing allows you to get a nice finished edge on your crumb fabric appliqué motifs. By stitching around your appliqué piece with the fusible side next to the fabric and then slitting in the centre and turning the shape through, you don't have to deal with all the seams created in your crumb fabric. Once turned, you can fuse the motif onto your background fabric (see The Crumb Quilting Method, Appliqué with made crumb fabric).

Fusible web can be used when adhering a single (not crumb) fabric to a background. Adding a decorative stitch around the raw edges will give the motif more durability.

Handy extras

A Purple Thang (a plastic tool), a craft stick and/or a capped pen are useful for running around the edges of your appliqué motifs when they have been turned through, as doing this helps to give the shape a crisp edge and defined points. A glue stick is great for holding motifs in place before securing by sewing.

Fabrics, threads and wadding (batting)

Using high-quality products will give your finished quilt a beautiful look and ensure that it lasts.

NOTE **The projects in this book assume a minimum usable width of fabric of 42in (107cm).**

Background and backing fabrics

Background fabrics should be good-quality quilting cottons. I used a lot of solids for the projects in this book, but you can mix up your backgrounds by using different colours. While white is clean and easy to match with your made crumb fabrics, using a coloured background can add something unexpected to your quilt. Other ways to do this are to use a small-scale print, or low-volume or tone-on-tone background fabrics.

For backing fabrics, good-quality quilting cottons are also ideal. Some fabric ranges come in extra-wide widths especially for backings, which may save you having to join pieces. Or you may wish to carry the scrappy theme to the back of your quilt and use larger leftovers to create a backing fabric of the required size.

Scrap and crumb fabrics

These too should be good-quality quilting cottons. Though, sometimes I throw linens and cotton lawns (finer cottons) into my made crumb fabrics, so do experiment. Scraps should be at least 1in in any one direction, but no bigger than 5in, unless it's a skinny strip when 8 to 10in long is fine. Using a variety of colours will give your made crumb fabric greater interest. You may wish to use all bright fabrics or all muted fabrics in a made crumb-fabric piece, or you could mix them. If you like the effect you are creating, go for it – there are no rules, only guidelines. When creating made crumb fabric in a single colourway make sure you include a wide range of values (i.e. light and dark shades) to add interest.

When making crumb fabric, baskets or tubs are useful for sorting and holding your scraps as you work, as it keeps them contained but allows you to easily find that next perfect piece.

Threads

High-quality 50-weight cotton thread in a neutral colour is best for creating your crumb fabric. When piecing, you can match the thread with your background fabric/s or continue with neutral thread.

Wadding (batting)

This is the middle layer of your quilt that goes between the quilt top and the backing fabric. Waddings are made from different materials, such as polyester, cotton, cotton-poly blends, wool, silk and bamboo. Cotton wadding will shrink slightly when washed, so, if you don't pre-wash it, it will give your quilt a crinkly softness when the quilt is laundered. I generally use a low-loft cotton-poly blend wadding as it is easy for me to machine quilt. Loft is the thickness of the wadding – the lower the loft, the thinner the wadding. Try out different waddings to find which works best for you.

THE CRUMB QUILTING METHOD

Welcome to the crumb quilting method. It is a fun and creative way to add interest to your quilts. Sewing even the tiniest of scraps together eliminates waste and results in one-of-a-kind fabrics to use in your quilting projects.

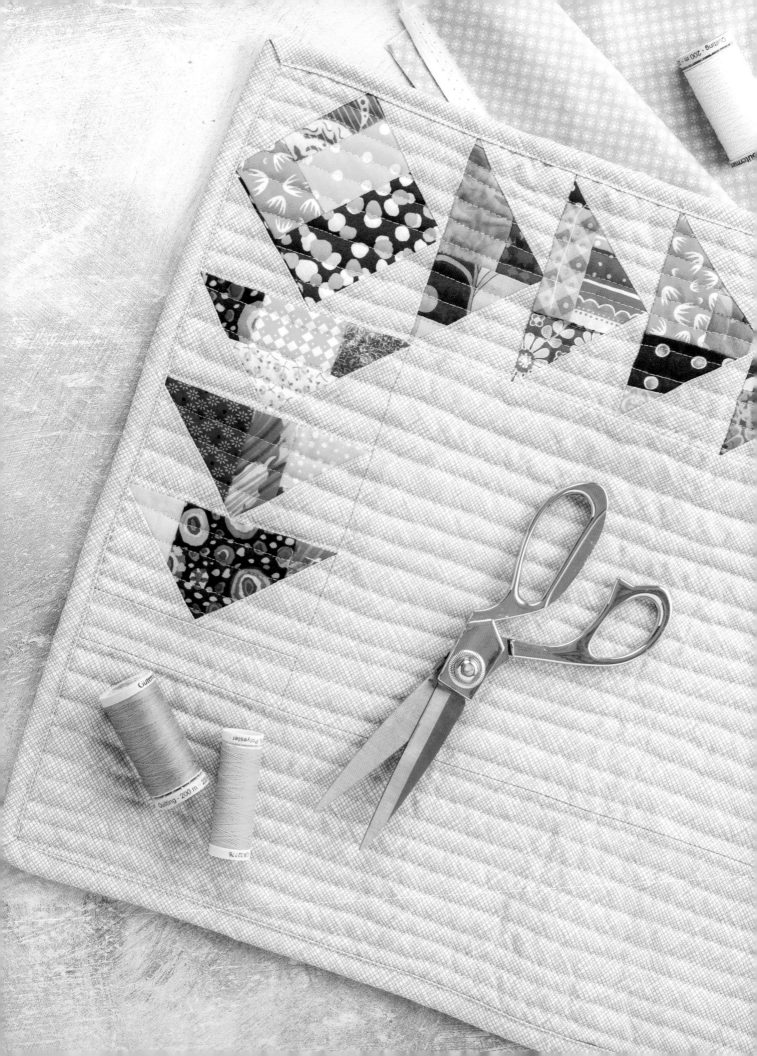

MAKING CRUMB FABRIC

1 Find two similar-sized scraps. If they don't have a straight edge, cut one. Place the scraps right sides together and sew along the straight edge. Open out and press.

2 Straighten up the edges as needed.

3 For odd-shaped pieces, you can overlap them slightly and cut a straight edge to sew along.

4 I like to save triangular-shaped scraps in a pile, ready to sew together when I find two of a similar size and shape.

5 Chain piece four or five of these units through your machine.

6 Find a scrap that will fit along one edge of your pressed and trimmed two-piece unit.

7 Place right sides together and sew.

8 Continue to add scraps around the edge of the made crumb fabric as it is formed, in a Log Cabin or Rail Fence fashion.

9 As units get bigger, sew two similar-sized units together.

10 Continue this process until the made crumb fabric reaches the desired size. Before trimming to size, spray with starch to make it more stable.

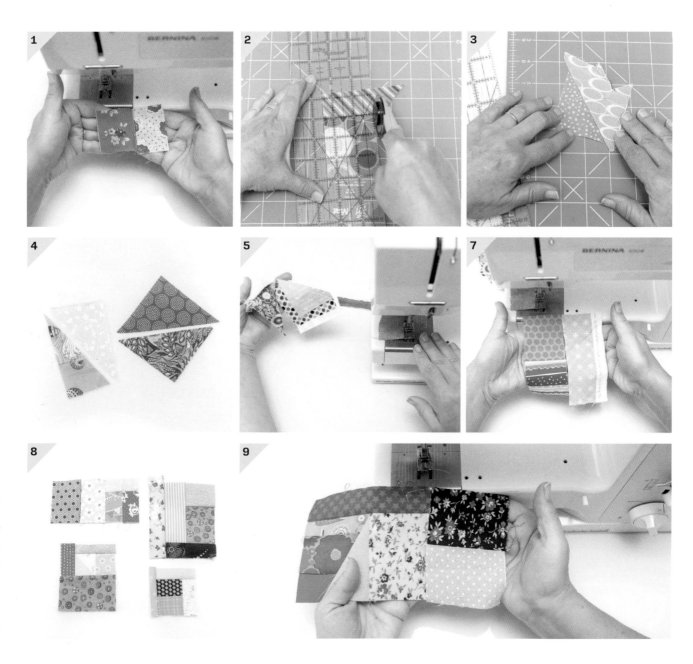

MAKING CRUMB-FABRIC BACKGROUNDS

11 For pieces smaller than 3in square, use scraps rather than crumb fabric. Using lots of different fabrics will give the crumb-fabric effect without having to deal with lots of seams.

12 When making crumb fabric for larger background pieces, feel free to use larger scraps. It will look great to have small pieces thrown in, but it will take a lot of time to make all of the background with tiny crumbs.

13 Once the crumb fabric reaches the desired size, spray with starch to stabilize it before trimming to size.

TIP **Avoid bulky seams near trimmed edges. If your cut is within ¼in of a seam unpick or cut away excess piece of fabric.**

APPLIQUÉ WITH MADE CRUMB FABRIC

14 Trace your shapes onto lightweight fusible interfacing.

15 Cut the shapes out roughly.

16 Place the fusible side of the interfacing shape against the right side of your made crumb fabric. Move the shape around until you get the look you are after. Feel around the edge of

your shape to ensure there aren't bulky seams and adjust the shape's position as necessary to avoid this.

17 Stitch on the drawn line of the shape.

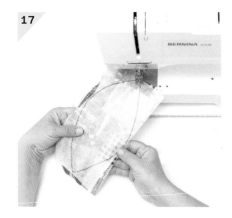

THE CRUMB QUILTING METHOD

18 Trim ¼in beyond the stitched line.

19 Trim the points, taking care not to nick the seam.

20 Pull interfacing away from the made crumb fabric.

21 Cut a slit in the centre of the interfacing only.

22 Turn right side out through the slit.

23 Use your favourite tool to run along the inside edge to make it crisp. I use a capped pen.

24 Arrange the shapes as required onto your background fabric. Press to fuse in place.

25 Topstitch or blanket stitch in place.

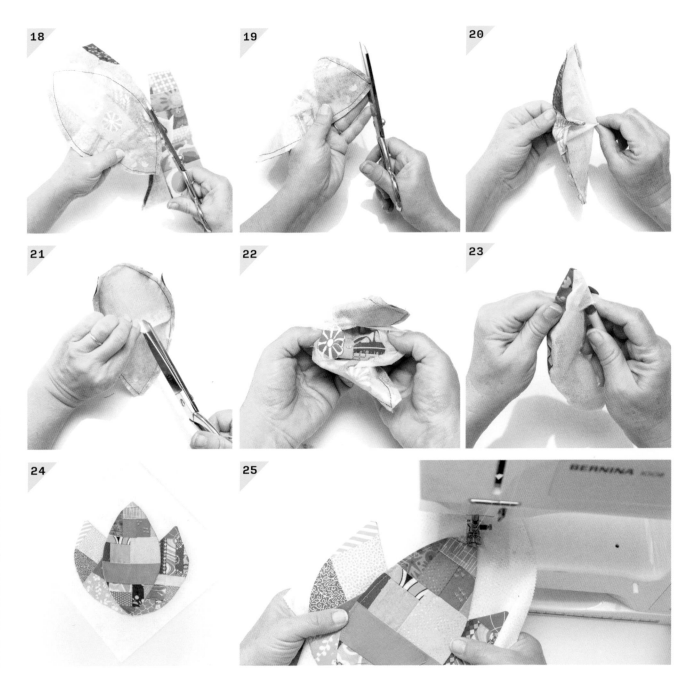

THE CRUMB QUILTING METHOD

REVERSE APPLIQUÉ WITH MADE CRUMB FABRIC

26 Mark and then cut out shapes from your background fabric. If you are going to use needleturn appliqué, cut ¼in inside the marked line. If you are going to use blanket stitch, cut on the marked line.

27 Place made crumb fabric beneath the cut shape and move it around until you get the look you desire. Feel around the edge of your shape to ensure there are no bulky seams and adjust the made fabric's position as necessary to avoid this.

28 Pin or glue the background fabric in place over the made crumb fabric.

29 Appliqué in your desired method.

Hand blanket stitch appliqué

30 To start, bring your needle up at a point just on the crumb-fabric side of the shape.

31 About ¼in from this point, take the needle back down into the background fabric, ¼in away from the edge of the shape.

32 Slide the needle underneath the fabric and bring the point of the needle up just on the crumb-fabric side opposite where you took the needle down. Bring your thread underneath the needle so as you pull it tight it catches and creates a line along the edge of the shape.

33 Repeat this process around the shape.

34 When going around points, make three stitches, one on each side and one at the point.

35 To finish, take your needle down at the same point where you started and tie off.

36 Carefully trim away excess made crumb fabric on the wrong side.

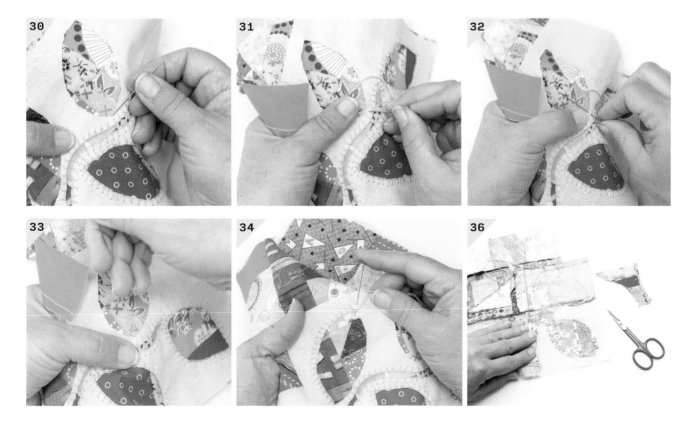

CRUMB BLOCK QUILTS

Using crumb fabric to create your blocks is a great way to add lots of variety and interest to a quilt. It also ensures a unique one-off scrappy look. So dig deep in your stash and let the fun begin!

TWIST AND SHOUT

Framing crumb-fabric blocks with a no-waste twisted border creates movement so the blocks dance across the quilt.

Approximate size: 67 x 59in (170 x 150cm)

MATERIALS

- 2¾yds (2.5m) of background and border fabric
- Fifty-six 6½in made crumb-fabric squares (see The Crumb Quilting Method, Making crumb fabric)
- 75 x 67in (190 x 170cm) of backing fabric
- ½yd (50cm) of binding fabric
- 75 x 67in (190 x 170cm) of wadding (batting)

Cutting instructions

Background and border fabric
- Fifty-six 3½ x 7in rectangles
- Fifty-six 3¼ x 9¼in rectangles
- Six 2in wide strips across the width of the fabric for borders

Binding fabric
- Seven 2½in wide strips across the width of the fabric

Twisted blocks

1 Take a 3½ x 7in background rectangle. Place it right side up and cut it on the diagonal as shown. Cut at least ¾in away from the corners.

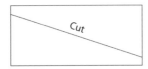

TIP When cutting the background rectangles, ensuring you cut at least ¾in from the corners, vary the distances so that you have cuts of different angles, which will give your blocks different degrees of twist.

2 Sew these pieces to the sides of a made crumb-fabric square as shown. Make sure you join the cut diagonal edges to the crumb-fabric square.

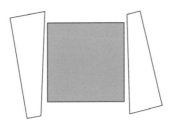

3 Straighten up the top and bottom edges level with the made crumb-fabric square as shown.

4 Take a 3¼ x 9¼in background rectangle and cut it on the diagonal as described in Step 1.

5 Sew these pieces to the top and bottom of the crumb-fabric square as shown, again making sure you join the cut diagonal edges to the crumb-fabric square.

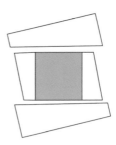

6 Square up your twisted block to 8½in square.

7 Repeat with your remaining made crumb-fabric squares and background rectangles to make fifty-six twisted blocks. Alternate the direction you cut the rectangles on the diagonal so that half of your blocks twist in one direction and half in the opposite direction.

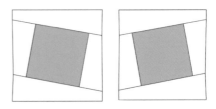

TIP If you place pairs of background rectangles wrong sides together you can make one cut to ensure that you have the pieces for two blocks that will twist in opposite directions to each other.

Quilt layout

8 Arrange the blocks into eight rows of seven blocks each, alternating the direction of twist.

9 Sew the blocks into rows and then join the rows.

Adding the border

10 Sew the border strips into one continuous length end to end. Subcut into two 2 x 64½in strips and two 2 x 59½in strips.

11 Sew the 2 x 64½in strips to the sides of the quilt top, and then sew the 2 x 59½in strips to the top and bottom.

Quilting and finishing

12 Make a quilt sandwich of the quilt top, the wadding (batting) and the backing fabric (see General Techniques, Making a quilt sandwich).

13 Quilt as desired. I quilted an eight-pointed star in the crumb-fabric square of each block and then echo quilted around the square. The remaining background space was quilted with swirls (see General Techniques, Quilting).

14 Square-up and bind to finish (see General Techniques, Squaring-up your quilt and Binding).

BEADED CURTAIN

I was thinking of beaded curtains when I made this quilt. My friend Ruth, who quilted it, saw lava lamps. Either way, it has a retro feel and a hippy vibe.

Approximate size: 90 x 77in (230 x 196cm)

MATERIALS

- 5¼yds (4.8m) of background fabric (includes binding)
- Enough made crumb fabric to cut one hundred and forty Wedge templates (see Made crumb-fabric wedges)
- 98 x 85in (250 x 216cm) of backing fabric
- 98 x 85in (250 x 216cm) of wadding (batting)

TIP If you would like to use a contrasting binding, then you will need 4⅜yd (4m) of background fabric and ⅞yd (80cm) of binding fabric.

Cutting instructions

Background fabric

- Thirteen 8½in wide strips across the width of the fabric. Subcut into one hundred and fifty Wedge templates

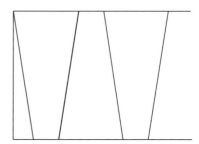

- Eight 5½in wide strips across the width of the fabric for borders
- Nine 2½in wide strips across the width of the fabric for binding

Made crumb-fabric wedges

1 Make around forty 8½ x 10–12in crumb-fabric rectangles (see The Crumb Quilting Method, Making crumb fabric).

2 Cut as many Wedge templates as you can from one crumb-fabric rectangle. Sew any unused rectangle to the next crumb-fabric rectangle on the 8½in edge and then cut as many Wedge templates as you can from this new rectangle.

3 Continue working in the same way until you have one hundred and forty Wedge templates. If required, make a few more 8½ x 10–12in crumb-fabric rectangles.

Quilt centre

4 Take one background Wedge template and one made crumb-fabric Wedge template. Place the background piece right side up, with the wider end at the top. With its narrower end at the top, place the made crumb-fabric piece right side down to top, matching up the edges as shown. Make sure the crumb-fabric piece is placed with its top right-hand corner ¼in below the top right-hand corner of the background piece.

¼in

5 Sew together. Flip open and press the seam towards the background fabric.

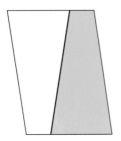

6 Repeat Steps 4 and 5 to make a total of fourteen identical background/made crumb-fabric pairs.

7 Join the pairs and then, with its wider end at the top, add a background Wedge template to the right-hand end of the row (i.e. to a made crumb-fabric Wedge). This completes one row.

8 Repeat Steps 4–7 to make a total of ten rows.

9 Take two rows. Invert the lower one so that the narrower ends of the background pieces meet and the wider ends of the made crumb-fabric pieces meet. Sew together.

10 Repeat Step 9 to make a total of five paired rows.

11 Making sure you match up the wider ends of the background pieces and the narrower ends of the made crumb-fabric pieces, join the paired rows to create the quilt centre.

12 Square up the side edges of the quilt centre, cutting level with outer points of the narrower ends of the background pieces that are at the end of each row.

Cut to square up edge   Cut to square up edge

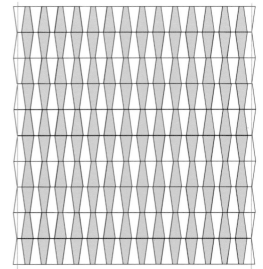

Borders

13 Sew the border strips into one continuous length end to end. Subcut into two 5½ x 80½in strips (side borders) and two 5½ x 77½in strips (top and bottom borders).

14 Sew the 5½ x 80½in strips to the sides of the quilt top, and then sew the 5½ x 77½in strips to the top and bottom.

TIP **If you prefer, before cutting your border strips you could measure your quilt top to determine the length of strips required. For the side border strips, measure down the centre of the quilt from outer top edge to outer bottom edge and cut your side border strips to this length. Once you have added the side border strips, measure across the centre of the quilt from outer side edge to outer side edge and cut your top and bottom border strips to this length.**

Quilting and finishing

15 Make a quilt sandwich of the quilt top, the wadding (batting) and the backing fabric (see General Techniques, Making a quilt sandwich).

16 Quilt as desired. My quilt was long-arm quilted with a bubble pattern (see General Techniques, Quilting).

17 Square-up and bind to finish (see General Techniques, Squaring-up your quilt and Binding).

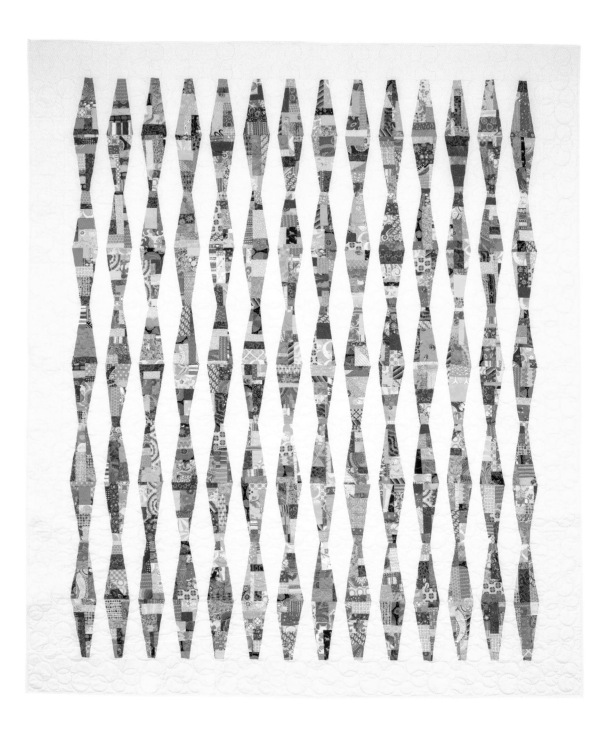

ZOODLES

The squiggly crumb-fabric shapes in these blocks remind me of wavy pasta, so it seemed fitting to call this quilt Zoodles.

Approximate size: 72 x 64in (183 x 163cm)

MATERIALS

- 5yds (4.6m) of background fabric (includes binding)
- Enough made crumb fabric to cut seventy-two 3½ x 10in rectangles (see The Crumb Quilting Method, Making crumb fabric)
- 80 x 72in (203 x 183cm) of backing fabric
- 80 x 72in (203 x 183cm) of wadding (batting)

> TIP **If you would like to use a contrasting binding, then you will need 4⅜yd (4m) of background fabric and ⅝yd (60cm) of binding fabric.**

Cutting instructions

Background fabric

- Thirty-six 4¼in wide strips across the width of the fabric. Subcut into one hundred and forty-four 4¼ x 10in rectangles
- Eight 2½in wide strips across the width of the fabric for binding

Zoodles blocks

1 Take a 3½ x 10in made crumb-fabric rectangle and place it right side up on your cutting mat. Take a 4¼ x 10in background rectangle and, also placed right side up, overlap it 1¼in from the top edge of the made crumb-fabric rectangle.

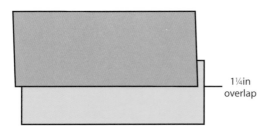

1¼in overlap

2 Use your rotary cutter to freehand cut a gentle curve through the overlapping area.

TIP **When cutting curves, don't make them too tight or they will be difficult to piece.**

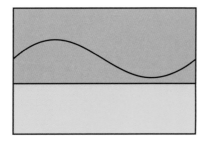

3 Discard the lower part of the background rectangle and the upper part of the made crumb-fabric rectangle, and then join the two remaining pieces along their newly-cut curved edges. Press.

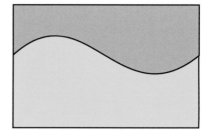

TIP **When sewing curved seams, with the pieces right sides together, start at one end of the curve and then sew slowly and smoothly along the curved edge, making sure edges match up. You may wish to pin the seam first, or you can bring the seams together as you stitch.**

4 Place the unit made in Step 3 right side up on your cutting mat. Take a 4¼ x 10in background rectangle and, also placed right side up, overlap it 1¼in from the bottom (made crumb fabric) straight edge of the unit.

5 Through the overlapping area, freehand cut a curve that is approximately parallel to the already-stitched curved seam. Discard the upper part of the background rectangle and the lower part of the unit made in Step 3, and then join the two remaining pieces along their newly-cut curved edges. Press.

6 Keeping the made crumb-fabric shape roughly centred, trim the unit made in Step 5 to 8½in square. This completes one zoodle block.

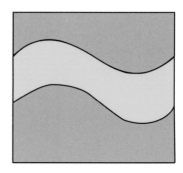

7 Repeat Steps 1–6 to make a total of seventy-two zoodle blocks.

Quilt layout

8 Arrange the blocks into nine rows of eight blocks each, alternating the orientation of the made crumb-fabric shape.

9 Sew the blocks into rows and then join the rows.

Quilting and finishing

10 Make a quilt sandwich of the quilt top, the wadding (batting) and the backing fabric (see General Techniques, Making a quilt sandwich).

11 Quilt as desired. My quilt was stitched with an allover pattern of swirls and circles (see General Techniques, Quilting).

12 Square-up and bind to finish (see General Techniques, Squaring-up your quilt and Binding).

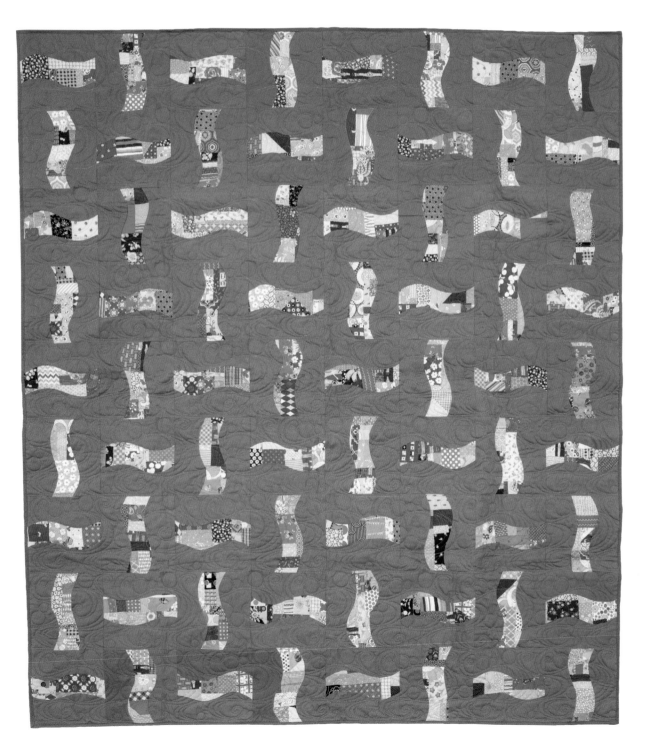

STAR FLOWER TABLE TOPPER

With vibrant star flowers and their stems and leaves simply popping on
a navy background, this topper will add life to any table setting.

Approximate size: 24in (61cm) square

MATERIALS

- ¾yd (70cm) of background fabric (includes binding)
- 1yd (1m) of ½in (12mm) wide bias tape
- Various crumb fabrics – see Cutting instructions
- ⅛yd (10cm) of lightweight fusible interfacing
- 28in (71cm) square of backing fabric
- 28in (71cm) square of wadding (batting)

> TIP **If you would like to use a contrasting binding, then you will need ½yd (50cm) of background fabric and ¼yd (30cm) of binding fabric.**

> TIP **If using a flying geese ruler: From a 2½in wide strip of background fabric, cut sixteen quarter-square triangles. From a 2½in wide strip of crumb fabric, cut thirty-two half-square triangles. Sew a half-square triangle to two adjacent sides of a quarter-square triangle to make a flying goose unit.**

Cutting instructions

Background fabric
- One 8½ x 24½in rectangle or three 8½in squares (see Step 9)
- Two 8½in squares
- Sixteen 2½ x 4½in rectangles
- Sixteen 2½in squares
- Three 2½in wide strips across the width of the fabric for binding

Crumb fabric
- Thirty-two 2½in squares
- Four 4½in squares
- Two approximately 10in green squares for leaves

> TIP **For small background and print pieces, you may find it easier to use scraps (crumb fabric) rather than made crumb fabric. Using lots of different fabrics will give the made crumb-fabric effect without having to deal with lots of seams.**

Interfacing
- Eight Leaf templates – cut the shapes out roughly, at least ¼in beyond the traced line (see The Crumb Quilting Method, Appliqué with made crumb fabric)

Star blocks

1 Take two 2½in crumb-fabric squares and a 2½ x 4½in background rectangle. On the wrong side of each square mark a diagonal line from corner to corner.

2 Working on one corner at a time, place a square on one corner of the rectangle, with the diagonal line running from the bottom corner to the top edge. Stitch on the marked line.

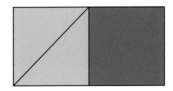

3 Trim ¼in beyond the stitched line then flip the corner open and press. Repeat for the other corner. This completes one flying goose unit.

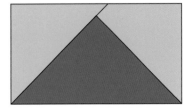

4 Repeat Steps 1–3 to make a total of sixteen flying geese units.

5 Take one 4½in crumb-fabric square, four 2½in background squares and four flying geese units. Arrange as shown.

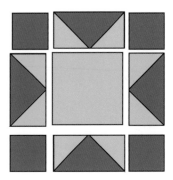

6 Join the units into rows and then join the rows to complete one star block.

7 Repeat Steps 5 and 6 to make a total of four star blocks.

Quilt layout

8 Sew an 8½in background square between two star blocks. Repeat.

9 Sew the 8½ x 24½in background rectangle between the two star rows. If you are using three 8½in squares, join the squares into a row and then sew this unit between the two star rows.

10 Place the fusible side of an interfacing leaf against the right side of one of the 10in green made crumb-fabric squares. Place the leaf so you will be able to make several leaves from the crumb-fabric square (you will need both 10in squares to make all of your leaves). Stitch on the drawn line and then trim ¼in beyond the stitched line.

11 Pull the interfacing away from the made crumb fabric and cut a slit in the centre of the interfacing only. Turn the leaf right side out through the slit and then run your favourite tool around the inside edge to make it crisp.

> TIP **For more details about making the leaves, see The Crumb Quilting Method, Appliqué with made crumb fabric. To make the inside edge of the leaf crisp, I like to use a craft stick or a capped pen, but use whichever tool works best for you.**

12 Repeat Steps 10 and 11 to make a total of eight leaves.

13 Cut the bias tape into two 18in lengths.

> TIP **You can buy pre-made ½in wide bias tape or you can make your own using a ½in bias tape maker. Full instructions come with the bias maker, but note that you will need to cut strips on the diagonal (i.e. at 45 degrees) of your fabric as this has the greatest stretch and will enable you to create curvy stems. You can use a single fabric, but I joined bias strips of different fabrics to create a scrappy stem.**

14 Referring to the flat shot, arrange your bias-tape stems and leaves on the quilt top. Pin or glue the stems in place and press the leaves to fuse them in position. To secure, topstitch just inside each long edge of the stems and around the edge of each leaf. To hide the raw ends of the stems, you can fold

the ends under before stitching in place. Alternatively, unpick the seam of the star block where you want the bias tape to go, insert the end of the tape in the gap created and then re-stitch the seam, trapping the bias tape in place as you do so.

Quilting and finishing

15 Make a quilt sandwich of the quilt top, the wadding (batting) and the backing fabric (see General Techniques, Making a quilt sandwich).

16 Quilt as desired. My topper was quilted with a tight stipple in the background. A dogwood flower was quilted in the centre of each star. Finally, ¼in echo quilting was done inside each star and leaf, and along each edge of the stems (see General Techniques, Quilting).

17 Square-up and bind to finish (see General Techniques, Squaring-up your quilt and Binding).

LOVE PILLOW

Love can be messy and often requires forgiveness, yet it is one of the most wonderful things on earth. How better to represent that than in crumb-created letters.

Approximate size: 19¼ x 32¾in (49 x 83cm)

MATERIALS

- ¾yd (70cm) of background fabric
- Various crumb fabric and made crumb-fabric pieces – see Cutting instructions
- 24 x 38in (61 x 96cm) of wadding (batting), optional – see Step 13
- ¾yd (70cm) of pillow back fabric
- ¾yd (70cm) of 1in (25mm) wide sew-on Velcro tape
- One standard bed pillow

Cutting instructions

Background fabric

- Three 1½ x 12½in rectangles
- Five 2½in squares
- One 2½ x 8½in rectangle
- Two 3½ x 4½in rectangles
- One 3½ x 10½in rectangle
- Two 3½ x 12½in rectangles
- Two 4½ x 34in rectangles
- One 5 x 13½in rectangle

Crumb fabric and made crumb fabric

- Four 1½in squares
- One 2½in square
- One 2½ x 5½in rectangle
- Four 2½ x 6½in rectangles
- Three 2½ x 8½in rectangles
- One 2½ x 10½in rectangle
- Two 2½ x 15in rectangles

TIP **For small crumb-fabric pieces it is easier to use scraps rather than made crumb fabric, as this avoids having to deal with lots of seams.**

Pillow back fabric

- Two 12½ x 33¼in rectangles

L block

1 Sew the 3½ x 10½in background rectangle to the right-hand side of 2½ x 10½in crumb-fabric rectangle. Sew the 2½ x 5½in crumb-fabric rectangle to the bottom (a 5½in edge) of this unit. This completes the letter 'L'.

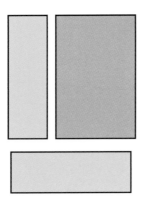

O block

2 Take the four 1½in crumb-fabric squares and draw a diagonal line from corner to corner on the wrong side of each one. Take the 2½ x 8½in background rectangle and place it right side up. Right sides together, place a square on one corner with the drawn line running from outer edge to outer edge of the rectangle. Sew on the drawn line. Press open and then trim the seam allowance. Repeat for each of the remaining corners. These are called sew-and-flip corners. You have now created the centre of the letter 'O'.

3 Sew a 2½ x 8½in crumb rectangle to each side (the 8½in edges) of the letter 'O' centre.

4 Take two 2½in background squares and draw a diagonal line from corner to corner on the wrong side of each one. Take a 2½ x 6½in crumb rectangle. Following the method described in Step 2, sew-and-flip a background square to each end of the crumb rectangle. Repeat to make a second unit.

5 Sew the units made in Step 4 to the top and bottom of the unit made in Step 3. This completes the letter 'O'.

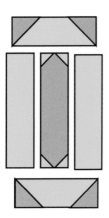

V block

6 Take the 5 x 13½in background rectangle and place it right side up on your cutting mat. Cut ¾in in from the top left corner to the centre of the bottom edge (a 5in edge). Then cut ¾in in from the top right corner to the centre of the bottom edge. Keep the pieces arranged as cut.

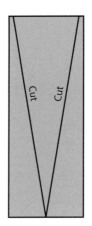

7 Sew a 2½ x 15in crumb rectangle to the newly-cut edge of the left-hand background triangle, making sure the rectangle extends ½in beyond the top of the triangle and that it also extends beyond the triangle's bottom edge. Then sew the centre background triangle to the other long edge of the crumb rectangle, making sure the rectangle extends ¼in at the top point of the centre triangle – the rectangle will also extend beyond the bottom point of the triangle. In the same manner, sew the remaining 2½ x 15in crumb rectangle to the other long edge of the centre triangle. Then sew the newly-cut edge of the right-hand background triangle to the other long edge of the crumb rectangle.

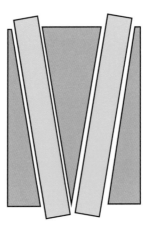

8 Square up the unit made in Step 7 to 8 x 12½in by first straightening up the bottom edge, then trimming the side edges and finally cutting the excess fabric from the top edge. This completes the letter 'V'.

E block

9 Sew a 2½in background square to the right-hand edge of a 2½in crumb square. Sew a 3½ x 4½in background rectangle to the top and bottom of this unit.

10 Sew a 2½ x 8½in crumb rectangle to the left-hand side of the unit made in Step 9.

11 Sew a 2½ x 6½in crumb rectangle to the top and bottom edges of the unit made in Step 10. This completes the letter 'E'.

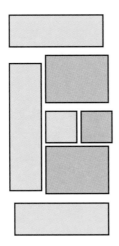

Creating the pillow top

12 Arrange the letters to spell 'LOVE'. Sew a 1½ x 12½in background rectangle between the letters. Sew a 3½ x 12½in background rectangle to each end of the word. Then sew a 4½ x 34in background rectangle to the top and bottom of the word.

13 You can quilt the pillow top. Layer the pillow top with wadding and quilt as desired. My pillow was quilted with rows of vines stitched at an angle of 45 degrees – the leaves are hearts and each vine has been separated by a single quilted line.

14 Trimming evenly, square up the pillow top to 19¾ x 33¼in.

Completing the pillow

15 Take the 12½ x 33¼in pillow back rectangles. On one long edge of each rectangle, turn under ¼in to the wrong side and press, then turn over 1¾in and press again. Topstitch in place along the folded edge.

16 Take one pillow back piece and place it right side up. Centre the hook side of the Velcro tape along the folded edge, approximately ⅛in in from the fold. Pin to secure and then stitch in place.

17 Take the remaining pillow back piece and place it wrong side up. Centre the loop side of the Velcro tape along the folded edge, approximately ⅛in in from the fold. Pin to secure and then stitch in place.

18 Place the pillow top right side up. Right side down and matching up the raw edges, place the pillow back piece made in Step 17 (loop side of the tape) on top, with the Velcro edge running across the centre. In the same way, place the pillow back piece made in Step 16 (hook side of the tape) in place. The pillow back pieces should overlap and the Velcro hooks and loops should match up.

19 Pin all around to secure. Take extra care where the pillow back pieces overlap and make sure the Velcro pieces match up. Sew all around with a ¼in seam. For extra strength, you could sew a second row of stitching where the pillow back pieces overlap.

20 Trim the corners, taking care not to nick the seam. Turn right side out through the overlapped edges. Insert a pillow, plump up and then close the Velcro fastening.

FLYING GEESE RUNNER

Crumb geese fly from opposite corners to create a contemporary table runner, which will add a sophisticated and stylish touch to any home.

Approximate size: 15 x 40in (38 x 102cm)

MATERIALS

- 1yd (1m) of background fabric (includes binding)
- Various crumb fabrics – see Cutting instructions
- 19 x 44in (48 x 112cm) of backing fabric
- 19 x 44in (48 x 112cm) of wadding (batting)

> TIP **If you would like to use a contrasting binding, then you will need ¾yd (70cm) of background fabric and ¼yd (30cm) of binding fabric.**

Cutting instructions

Background fabric

- One 7½ x 32½in rectangle
- Two 4½ x 18½in rectangles
- Four 2⅞in squares
- Forty-eight 2½in squares
- Two 1½ x 4½in rectangles
- Three 2½in wide strips across the width of the fabric for binding

Crumb fabric

- Two 3⅜in squares
- Twenty-four 2½ x 4½in rectangles

> TIP **For details about how to make crumb fabric, see The Crumb Quilting Method, Making crumb fabric. For small background and print pieces, you may find it easier to use scraps (crumb fabric) rather than made crumb fabric. Using lots of different fabrics will give the made crumb-fabric effect without having to deal with lots of seams.**

TIP If you prefer, you can make your flying geese units using a flying geese ruler. From a 2½in wide strip of crumb fabric, use the ruler to cut twenty-four quarter-square triangles. If you don't have a long strip of crumb fabric, just use smaller 2½in wide pieces to cut the number of quarter-square triangles required. From a 2½in wide strip of background fabric, use the ruler to cut forty-eight half-square triangles. Sew a half-square triangle to two adjacent sides of a quarter-square triangle to make a flying goose unit.

Flying geese units

1 Take two 2½in background squares and a 2½ x 4½in crumb fabric rectangle. On the wrong side of each square mark a diagonal line from corner to corner.

2 Working on one corner at a time, place a square on one corner of the rectangle, with the diagonal line running from the bottom corner to the top edge. Stitch on the marked line.

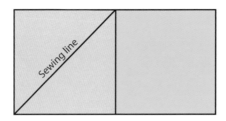

3 Trim ¼in beyond the stitched line then flip the corner open and press. Repeat for the other corner. This completes one flying goose unit.

Square-in-a-square units

5 Take two 2⅞in background squares and cut each once on the diagonal to give four triangles.

6 Take a 3⅜in crumb fabric square and sew a background triangle to each side in the order shown.

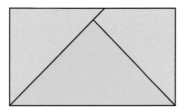

4 Repeat Steps 1–3 to make a total of twenty-four flying geese units.

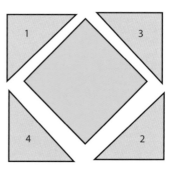

7 Keeping the square centred, trim to 4½in square. This completes one square-in-a-square unit.

8 Repeat Steps 5–7 to make a total of two square-in-a-square units.

Runner layout
Follow the layout diagram when constructing the runner top.

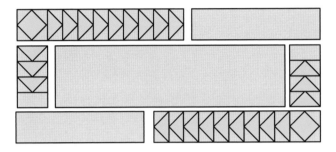

9 Take three flying geese units and sew into a strip on their 4½in edges, making sure all the geese are flying in the same direction. Sew a 1½ x 4½in background rectangle to the top of the strip, i.e. to the point of a goose. Repeat.

10 Sew the units made in Step 9 to the short edges of the 7½ x 32½in background rectangle, making sure the geese are flying downwards on the left-hand edge and are flying upwards on the right-hand edge.

11 Take nine flying geese units and sew into a strip on their 4½in edges, making sure all the geese are flying in the same direction. Sew a square-in-a-square unit to the bottom of the strip, i.e. to the 4½in edge of the goose. Sew a 4½ x 18½in background rectangle to the top of the strip, i.e. to the point of a goose. Repeat.

12 Sew the units made in Step 11 to the long edges of the unit made in Step 10, making sure the geese are flying towards the right on the top edge and are flying towards the left on the bottom edge. In each case, the square-in-a-square unit will match up with the bottom of the flying geese strip on the sides of the runner. This completes the runner top.

Quilting and finishing
13 Make a quilt sandwich of the runner top, the wadding (batting) and the backing fabric (see General Techniques, Making a quilt sandwich).

14 Quilt as desired. My runner was quilted with organic parallel lines across the width (40in edge) of the quilt (see General Techniques, Quilting).

15 Square-up and bind to finish (see General Techniques, Squaring-up your quilt and Binding).

APPLIQUÉ WITH CRUMB FABRIC

Made crumb-fabric appliqué motifs are a simple way to give your work a fun twist, as well as adding lots of colours and interesting prints. Clever methods eliminate the worry of handling bulky seams, so relax and enjoy!

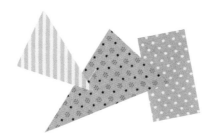

MARY'S GARDEN

My niece Mary has always loved to sew with me. When she was little she would gather up the scraps around my sewing room and design her own quilts on my design wall. In honour of her scrappy designs I created Mary's Garden.

Approximate size: 86 x 72in (220 x 183cm)

MATERIALS

- ⅞yd (80cm) of daisy background fabric
- 2¼yds (2.1m) of tulip background fabric
- 1⅜yds (1.2m) of sashing fabric
- Various crumb fabrics – see Tulip blocks
- Various scrappy prints – see Cutting instructions
- 4yds (3.7m) of 36in (90cm) wide or 6½yds (6m) of 20in (50cm) wide lightweight fusible interfacing
- 94 x 80in (240 x 203cm) of backing fabric
- ¾yd (70cm) of binding fabric
- 94 x 80in (240 x 203cm) of wadding (batting)

TIP When cutting out interfacing Templates C, D and D Reverse, cut the shapes out roughly, at least ¼in beyond the traced line (see The Crumb Quilting Method, Appliqué with made crumb fabric).

Cutting instructions

Daisy background fabric
- Twenty 7in squares

Tulip background fabric
- Thirty 10in squares

Sashing fabric
- One hundred and twenty 1½ x 9½in strips

Various scrappy prints
- Forty-eight 1½ x 22in strips
- Eighty 2in squares
- Two hundred and seventy-seven 2½in squares
- Seventy-one 1½in squares
- One hundred and sixty Template A
- Twenty Template B

Interfacing
- One hundred and sixty Template A
- Thirty Template C
- Thirty Template D
- Thirty Template D Reverse

Binding fabric
- Nine 2½in wide strips across the width of the fabric

Daisy blocks

1 Place the fusible side of an interfacing Template A on the right side of a scrappy print Template A. Using a scant ¼in seam, stitch around the curved edges of the petal only.

2 Using the opening along the bottom edge, turn the petal right side out.

> TIP **When turning the petals right side out, make a slit in the interfacing two thirds of the way up from the bottom. Place your thumb in the pocket between the interfacing and fabric, and your index finger at the top of the seam. Gently push your index finger down onto your thumb while using your other hand to pull the petal right side out. Run your turning tool around the edge to finish turning the petal.**

3 Use your favourite tool to run along the inside edge of the petal to make it crisp. I use a craft stick. Press.

4 Make eight of these petals.

5 Take a 7in daisy background square. Fold it in half lengthways and widthways. Lightly press to create guidelines.

6 Line up four of your petals over the vertical and horizontal guidelines as shown. Press to fuse in place and then topstitch around each petal.

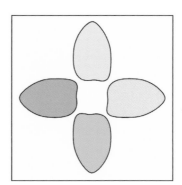

7 Centre the four remaining petals between the ones already sewn in position as shown. Press to fuse in place and then topstitch to secure.

8 Take a scrappy print Template B and, with the right side away from you, start folding the edge over to the wrong side by ¼in. Using a running stitch, sew around the edge of the circle through both layers. Pull thread tight and tie off to create a yo-yo.

> TIP **If you prefer, a Clover 'Quick' Yo-Yo Maker, size Small, could be used to make the daisy flower centres.**

9 Stitch the yo-yo to the centre of your daisy as shown.

10 Keeping the flower centred, square up your daisy square to 6½in square.

11 Make twenty daisy squares.

12 Sort your 1½ x 22in scrappy print strips into eight groups of six strips each.

13 Sew each group into a strip set (see General Techniques, Piecing, Strip piecing). Each strip set should measure 6½ x 22in.

14 Subcut the strip sets into eighty 2 x 6½in units.

15 Sew one of these units to the top and bottom of each of your daisy squares.

16 To the remaining units, sew a 2in scrappy print square to each end. Sew these units to the sides of your daisy squares.

17 Set aside your daisy blocks. Each one should measure 9½in square.

TIP **To create made crumb-fabric units such as rectangles, sew crumb squares and strips together in a Log Cabin and/or Rail Fence fashion until you have a made crumb-fabric piece of the required size. A picture tutorial for this can be found at: www.auntemsquilts.com/blog/fabric-from-scraps**

19 From each made crumb-fabric rectangle you will be able to make one each of Template C, D and D Reverse, so make sure you place the interfacing templates efficiently.

20 Place the fusible side of an interfacing Template C against the right side of a made crumb-fabric rectangle. Stitch on the drawn line and then trim ¼in beyond the stitched line. Repeat for an interfacing Template D and D Reverse.

21 Make a slit in the centre of the interfacing only and turn the shapes right side out through the slit.

22 Use your favourite tool to run along the inside edges to make them crisp. I use a craft stick for the edges and a pen lid for the points. Press.

23 Repeat Steps 20–22 with your remaining made crumb-fabric rectangles and interfacing Template Cs, and your Templates D and D Reverse.

24 Take a 10in tulip background square. Arrange a Template C, D and D Reverse to create a tulip.

25 Remove Template C. Press to fuse Templates D and D Reverse in place as shown and then topstitch to secure.

Tulip blocks

18 Use various crumb fabrics to create thirty 9 x 12in made crumb-fabric rectangles.

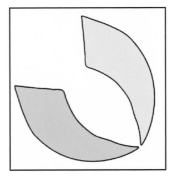

26 Replace Template C. Press to fuse in place as shown and then topstitch to secure.

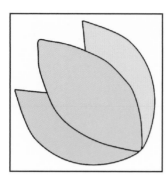

27 Keeping the flower centred, square up your tulip block to 9½in square.

28 Make thirty tulip blocks. Set aside.

Corner and setting triangles

29 Using your 2½in scrappy print squares, make eight strips of four squares each. Sew these into two four-by-four blocks as shown.

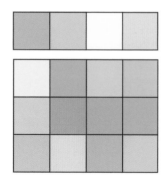

30 Cut each block once on the diagonal as shown.

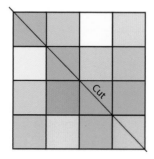

31 These are your four corner triangles. Set aside.

32 Use your remaining 2½in scrappy print squares to make thirty-five strips of seven squares each. Sew these into five seven-by-seven blocks as shown.

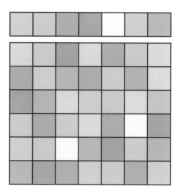

33 Cut each block twice on the diagonal as shown.

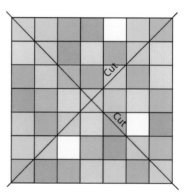

34 These are your setting triangles (you will have two extra). Set aside.

Quilt layout

35 Following On-point settings (see General Techniques, Piecing), sew your daisy and tulip blocks, sashing strips, 1½in scrappy print squares, and corner and setting triangles together. Your quilt top is now complete.

Quilting and finishing

36 Make a quilt sandwich of the quilt top, the wadding (batting) and the backing fabric (see General Techniques, Making a quilt sandwich).

37 Quilt as desired. I echo quilted around each flower and then stitched a tight stipple in the backgrounds to make the flowers pop (see General Techniques, Quilting).

38 Square-up and bind to finish (see General Techniques, Squaring-up your quilt and Binding).

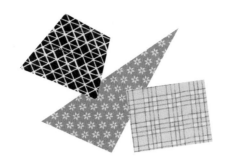

LOOSE CHANGE

Appliquéd circles are set on-point in this token man quilt,
which was made in honour of my husband and sons.

Approximate size: 81 x 68in (206 x 173cm)

MATERIALS

- Fifty 10in precut squares or 3¾yds (3.5m) of background fabric
- Fifty 10in made crumb-fabric squares
- 2¼yds (2m) for triangles and binding fabric
- 3yds (2.8m) of 36in (90cm) or 6yds (5.5m) of 20in (50cm) wide lightweight interfacing
- 89 x 76in (226 x 193cm) of backing fabric
- 89 x 76in (226 x 193cm) of wadding (batting)

Cutting instructions

Background fabric
- Fifty 10in squares

Triangles and binding fabric
- Five 14¾in squares for setting triangles
- Two 7¾in squares for corner triangles
- Eight 2½in wide strips across the width of the fabric for binding

Interfacing
- Fifty Circle templates – cut the shapes out roughly, at least ¼in beyond the traced line (see The Crumb Quilting Method, Appliqué with made crumb fabric)

Circle blocks

1 Place the fusible side of an interfacing circle against the right side of a made crumb-fabric square. Stitch on the drawn line and then trim ¼in beyond the stitched line.

2 Pull the interfacing away from the made crumb fabric and cut a slit in the centre of the interfacing only. Turn the circle right side out through the slit and then run your favourite tool around the inside edge to make it crisp.

> TIP **To make the inside edge of the circles crisp, I like to use a craft stick or a capped pen, but use whichever tool works best for you.**

3 Take the made crumb-fabric circle. Fold it into quarters and pinch just the edges to make short guidelines.

4 Take a 10in background square. Fold it in half lengthways and widthways. Lightly press to create guidelines. Place the square right side up and then, also right side up, place the made crumb-fabric circle centrally on top, using the guidelines to help you position it.

5 Press to fuse in position and then topstitch in place. This completes one circle block.

6 Repeat Steps 1–5 to make a total of fifty circle blocks.

> TIP **To create interest and add movement, when placing the circles onto the background squares, arrange them so the orientations of the seams of the made crumb fabric run in different directions relative to the edges of the squares (see flat shot).**

Quilt layout

7 Take the 14¾in setting-triangles squares and cut each twice on the diagonal to give twenty setting triangles (you will have two spare).

8 Take the 7¾in corner-triangles squares and cut each once on the diagonal to give four corner triangles.

9 Referring to the flat shot, arrange your circle blocks on-point into ten diagonal rows, with a corner triangle at each corner and setting triangles at the ends of the rows to fill in the jagged outer edges.

10 Sew the diagonal rows together, adding the corner triangles last. This completes your quilt top (see General Techniques, Piecing, On-point settings).

Quilting and finishing

11 Make a quilt sandwich of the quilt top, the wadding (batting) and the backing fabric (see General Techniques, Making a quilt sandwich).

12 Quilt as desired. Mine was quilted with a five-petal flower motif in each circle and an allover flame pattern in the backgrounds (see General Techniques, Quilting).

13 Square-up and bind to finish (see General Techniques, Squaring-up your quilt and Binding).

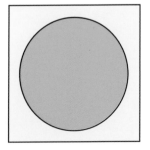

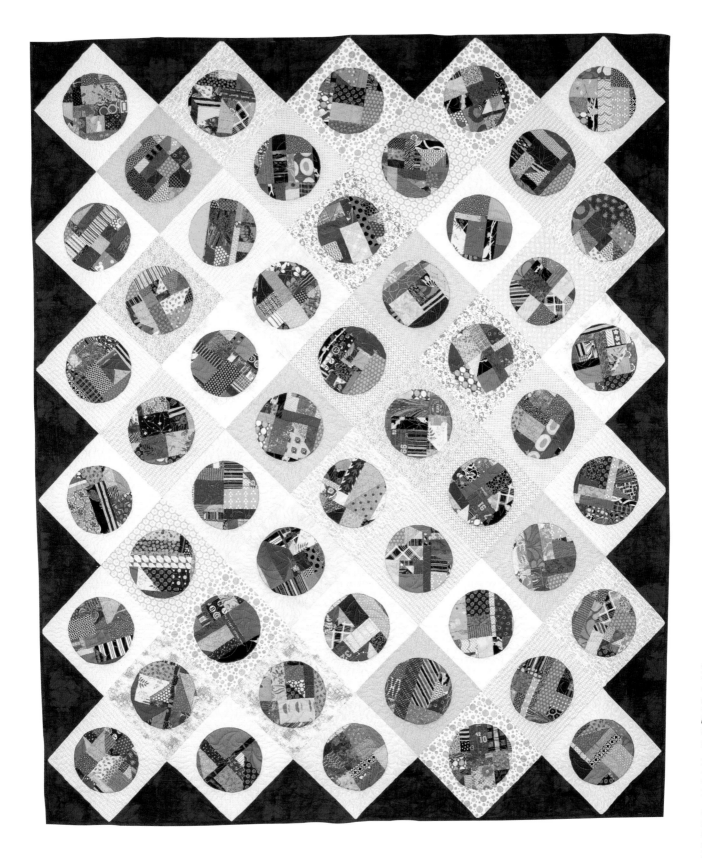

BLOWIN' IN THE WIND

A colourwash of crumb fabrics overlaid with a cut neutral
background is used to create a centre of multi-coloured leaves,
which is then surrounded by spinning pinwheels.

Approximate size: 44in (112cm) square

MATERIALS

- 1½yds (1.4m) of background fabric
- Various scrappy prints – see Cutting instructions
- Various crumb fabrics – see Cutting instructions
- 52in (132cm) square of backing fabric
- ⅜yd (40cm) of binding fabric
- 52in (132cm) square of wadding (batting)

Cutting instructions

Background fabric
- One 18½in square
- Ninety-two 3½in squares

Scrappy prints
- Forty pairs of 3½in squares (i.e. eighty squares in total)
- Twelve single 3½in squares

Crumb fabrics
- One 6½in square in each of the following colours: mid-brown, light brown, dark green, light green, orange, pink, purple, red, yellow
- Two 2½ x 17½in strips
- Two 2½ x 21½in strips
- Two 2½ x 40½in strips
- Two 2½ x 44½in strips

TIP **For this project, if you prefer, you could make the strips of crumb fabrics from squares and/or rectangles, as this will avoid having bias edges in your border pieces, which could distort your quilt. I have used strips made from double rows of squares – the squares need to be cut 1½in square, so it's a great way to use up small scraps.**

Binding fabric
- Five 2½in wide strips across the width of the fabric

Quilt centre

1 Take your 6½in crumb squares and arrange them into a nine-patch layout, with the colours placed as shown. Sew the squares into rows and then sew the rows together.

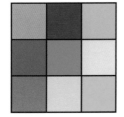

2 Take the 18½in background square. Referring to the flat shot for guidance, trace the Leaves templates onto the right side. Make sure the outer leaves are at least 1½in in from the edge of the square.

3 Cut out the leaf shapes. If you are going to use needleturn appliqué, cut ¼in inside the marked lines. If you are going to use blanket stitch appliqué, cut on the marked lines.

4 Both right side up, and referring to the flat shot for guidance, place the cut 18½in background square on top of the crumb fabric nine-patch unit. Pin, tack or glue the top fabric in place.

5 Appliqué around the cut shapes using your chosen method.

6 Keeping the design centred, trim to 17½in square.

7 Sew the 2½ x 17½in crumb strips to the top and bottom of the leaf unit. Then sew the 2½ x 21½in crumb strips to each side. Set aside.

Pinwheel units

8 Take two 3½in background squares and one pair of 3½in print squares. On the wrong side of the background squares, draw a diagonal line from corner to corner.

9 Take one background square and one print square. Place them right sides together with the marked square on top. Sew ¼in either side of the drawn line. Cut through both layers on the marked line.

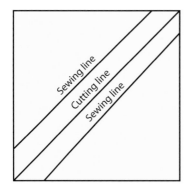

10 Open the units out and press. Keeping the 45-degree line of your ruler aligned with the diagonal seam, trim to 3in square. You will now have two identical half-square triangles.

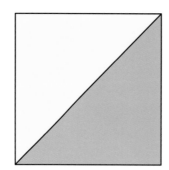

11 Repeat Steps 9 and 10 with the remaining background and print square. You will now have four identical half-square triangles.

12 Arrange the half-square triangles into two rows of two, making sure you orientate them as shown. Sew into rows and then sew the rows together. This completes one pinwheel block.

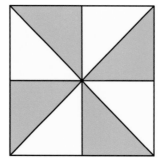

13 Repeat Steps 8–12 with your remaining pairs of 3½in print squares to make a total of forty pinwheel blocks. (You will have twelve 3½in background squares remaining.)

14 Take one of your remaining 3½in background squares. On the wrong side, draw a diagonal line from corner to corner.

15 Take one of your single 3½in print squares and, right sides together, place the marked background square on top. Sew ¼in on one side only of the drawn line. Cut through both layers on the marked line. Sew the liberated triangles to adjacent sides of the half-square triangle as shown (see overleaf). This completes one half-pinwheel block.

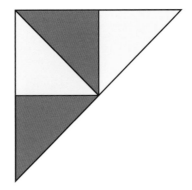

16 Repeat Steps 14 and 15 to make a total of twelve half-pinwheel blocks.

Quilt layout

17 Referring to the flat shot, arrange your pinwheel and half-pinwheel blocks into rows around the on-point quilt centre. The diagonal edges of the half-pinwheel blocks are next to the quilt centre.

TIP **If you have one, you will find a design wall useful for playing with arrangements of your blocks and half-blocks. If you don't have one, a large sheet pinned to a curtain works well as an alternative, or you could hang a large piece of wadding on the wall.**

18 The pinwheel units that will be joined to your quilt centre are constructed first. Referring to the diagram and working left to right, make the following rows: two pinwheel blocks and one half-pinwheel block; one pinwheel block and one half-pinwheel block; one half-pinwheel block. Join the rows. This completes one centre pinwheel unit.

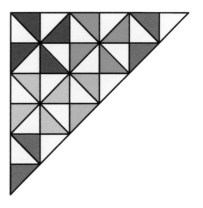

19 Make the three remaining centre pinwheel units in the same manner.

20 Sew the centre pinwheel units to the sides of the quilt centre. Join opposite sides first and then join the two remaining units.

21 Sew the top and bottom rows of eight pinwheel blocks each together. Set aside.

22 Sew the six pinwheel blocks at each side of the quilt centre into vertical rows. Sew these to each side of the quilt centre.

23 Sew the rows made in Step 21 to the top and bottom of the quilt centre.

24 Sew the 2½ x 40½in crumb strips to the sides of the quilt centre. Then sew the 2½ x 44½in crumb strips to the top and bottom. This completes the quilt top.

Quilting and finishing

25 Make a quilt sandwich of the quilt top, the wadding (batting) and the backing fabric (see General Techniques, Making a quilt sandwich).

26 Quilt as desired. Mine was quilted with a stipple pattern in the background of the leaf centre. The leaves were stitched in the ditch and a vein quilted in the centre of each one. A chain of leaves was quilted in the crumb borders. The pinwheel blocks were quilted with a starfish-like design, with wavy lines radiating out from the centre of the block (see General Techniques, Quilting).

27 Square-up and bind to finish (see General Techniques, Squaring-up your quilt and Binding).

OVER THE RAINBOW

Low-volume crumb fabrics are made into Drunkard's Path blocks with bright solids, and then arranged into a beautiful colourful rainbow.

Approximate size: 76½ x 67½in (194 x 172cm)

MATERIALS

- ⅜yd (40cm) each of three different pinks (P1–P3), oranges (O1–O3), yellows (Y1–Y3), greens (G1–G3), blues (B1–B3) and violets/purples (V1–V3)
- Sixty-four 10in low-volume made crumb-fabric squares
- 3⅝yds (3.4m) of 36in (90cm) or 7¼yds (6.7m) of 20in (50cm) wide lightweight interfacing
- 84 x 76in (214 x 193cm) of backing fabric
- ⅝yd (60cm) of binding fabric
- 84 x 76in (214 x 193cm) of wadding (batting)

> TIP **For details about how to make crumb fabric, see The Crumb Quilting Method, Making crumb fabric.**

Cutting instructions

Pinks, yellows, greens and blues

- Three 10in squares from each of one fabric of each colour
- Four 10in squares from each of the two remaining fabrics of each colour

You will have eleven 10in squares of each colour in total.

Oranges and violets/purples

- Four 10in squares from each of one fabric of each colour
- Three 10in squares from each of the two remaining fabrics of each colour

You will have ten 10in squares of each colour in total.

Interfacing

- Sixty-four Circle templates – cut the shapes out roughly, at least ¼in beyond the traced line (see The Crumb Quilting Method, Appliqué with made crumb fabric)

Binding fabric

- Eight 2½in wide strips across the width of the fabric

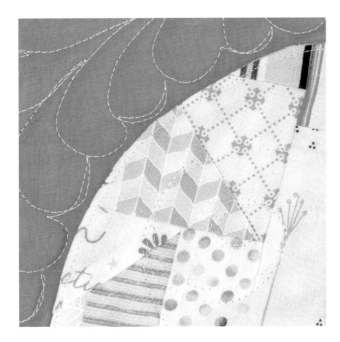

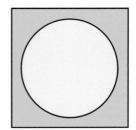

5 Press to fuse in position and then topstitch in place.

6 Cut the square into quarters as shown.

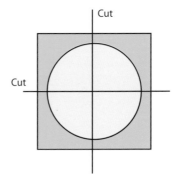

7 This gives you four Drunkard's Path blocks, each measuring 5in square.

Drunkard's Path blocks

1 Place the fusible side of an interfacing circle against the right side of a made crumb-fabric square. Stitch on the drawn line and then trim ¼in beyond the stitched line.

2 Pull the interfacing away from the made crumb fabric and cut a slit in the centre of the interfacing only. Turn the circle right side out through the slit and then run your favourite tool around the inside edge to make it crisp.

> TIP **For more details about making the circle blocks, see The Crumb Quilting Method, Appliqué with made crumb fabric. To make the inside edge of the circles crisp, I like to use a craft stick or a capped pen, but use whichever tool works best for you.**

3 Take the made crumb-fabric circle. Fold it into quarters and pinch just the edges to make short guidelines.

4 Take a 10in pink square. Fold it in half lengthways and widthways. Lightly press to create guidelines. Place the square right side up and then, also right side up, place the made crumb-fabric circle centrally on top, using the guidelines to help you position it.

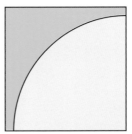

8 Repeat Steps 1–7 with your remaining low-volume made crumb-fabric squares and coloured squares to make a total of two hundred and fifty-six Drunkard's Path blocks.

Quilt layout

Follow the layout diagram when constructing the quilt top.

P1 P2 P1 P3 P2 P1 P1 O1 P3 P1 P2 P3 P3 P1 P2
P2 P3 P1 P2 O1 P3 P2 P3 P2 P2 P3 P1 P2 P3 P2
P3 O3 P2 O1 P1 P2 P1 O2 P3 O1 P1 P2 O2 P3 P1
O2 Y1 P3 P3 P2 O1 O2 P2 P3 O3 O2 P3 O3 O2 O1
Y2 O1 O3 O1 O2 Y1 O3 O2 O2 O1 O1 O2 O1 Y1 O3
O3 O3 Y1 Y2 O1 O2 O1 Y1 Y2 Y1 O3 O1 Y2 O2 O1
Y1 Y3 O3 Y3 Y2 O1 Y1 Y2 O3 Y2 Y1 G1 Y1 Y2 O3
Y2 Y2 Y3 Y1 Y2 Y3 Y2 Y1 Y3 G1 Y3 Y2 Y3 G1 Y2
G1 Y3 G2 Y3 G2 G1 Y3 G3 Y2 Y3 G2 Y2 G1 G3 Y3
G2 G3 Y3 G3 G2 Y3 G2 Y3 G1 G1 G2 Y3 G3 G1 G2
G3 G1 G2 G3 G1 G2 B1 G3 B2 G2 G3 G1 G2 G3 G3
G2 G3 B2 G2 G3 G3 B2 G2 B1 G3 B1 B2 B1 B3 B2
B2 B1 G2 B3 B2 B1 B3 B1 B3 B2 G3 B1 B2 B1 B1
B1 B3 B2 P2 V1 B2 B3 B2 B3 B1 B3 V1 B1 B3 V2
B3 V1 B1 B3 B3 V2 B1 V1 V3 V2 V1 V2 B3 V2 V1
V2 V3 B3 V2 V1 V1 V2 V3 V1 V1 V3 B3 V1 V3 B3
V1 V3 V1 V2 V2 V3 V3 V1 V3 V2 V1 V3 V2 V3 V1

9 Arrange your Drunkard's Path blocks into seventeen rows of fifteen blocks each as shown. Note the colour placements and orientations of the blocks. (You will have one violet/purple Drunkard's Path block spare.)

10 Sew the blocks into rows and then join the rows. This completes your quilt top.

Quilting and finishing

11 Make a quilt sandwich of the quilt top, the wadding (batting) and the backing fabric (see General Techniques, Making a quilt sandwich).

12 Quilt as desired. Mine was quilted with a continuous row of feathers through each diagonal created by the colour fabrics. The low-volume quarter-circle areas were quilted with swirls (see General Techniques, Quilting).

13 Square-up and bind to finish (see General Techniques, Squaring-up your quilt and Binding).

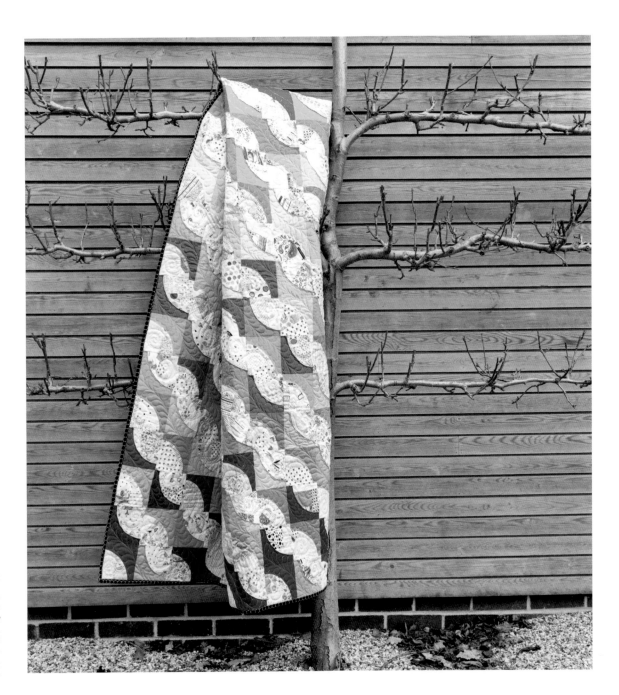

APPLIQUÉ WITH CRUMB FABRIC

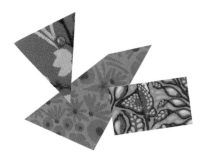

FLOWER PINCUSHION

A simple flower motif is jazzed up using reverse appliqué
and blanket stitch worked over made crumb fabric.

Approximate size: 6 x 3in (15 x 7.5cm)

MATERIALS

- Two 6½ x 3½in rectangles for pincushion front
  and back
- One 3½in bright floral made crumb-fabric square
- One 3½in green made crumb-fabric square
- Stranded cotton (embroidery floss) or perle
  (pearl) cotton to match crumb fabrics
- One button for flower centre
- Crushed walnut shells (walnut grit)

**TIP Crushed walnut shells (grit) are great
for filling pincushions as they are quite
weighty and are also abrasive, which
cleans and sharpens your pins. It is readily
available online and from some pet stores
as it's often used to line reptile vivaria.**

Pincushion front

1 Keeping the design centred, trace the Flower Pincushion
template onto the right side of one of the 6½ x 3½in
rectangles.

2 Cut out the flower and leaf shapes on the marked lines.

3 Sew the bright floral and green made crumb-fabric squares
together.

4 Both right side up, place the cut 6½ x 3½in rectangle on
top of the made crumb-fabric unit, with the bright floral
square underneath the flower shape and the green square
underneath the leaf shapes. Pin or glue the top fabric in place.

5 Appliqué around the cut shapes in blanket stitch (see The
Crumb Quilting Method, Hand blanket stitch appliqué). If you
wish, embroider a stem – I stitched mine in chain stitch.

Finishing

6 Place the pincushion front right sides together with the
remaining 6½ x 3½in rectangle. Pin all around to secure.

7 Sew all around with a ¼in seam, leaving a 1½–2in gap on
one long edge. To secure the seam, take a few backstitches at
the start and end of your stitching.

8 Clip the corners, taking care not to nick the seam. Turn right
side out through the gap.

9 Fill firmly with crushed walnut shells and blind stitch the
opening closed. Sew the button in the centre of the flower to
complete the pincushion.

CRUMB QUILT BACKGROUNDS

Why use one fabric when you can use many? A scrappy crumb background gives fabulous depth and interest to your quilts – and it's a great way to put a dent in your stash, too!

WONKY ROSE

A fun, funky play on the traditional Log Cabin block creates this Impressionist-style rose garden.

Approximate size: 66 x 55in (168 x 140cm)

MATERIALS

- 1yd (1m) of sashing fabric
- Rose fabrics (pink, purple, red, yellow and orange) – scrap strips, at least 1–2in (2.5–5cm) wide, totalling approximately ⅜yd (40cm) of each colour
- Rose centre fabrics (I used brown prints) – scraps totalling approximately ¼yd (30cm)
- Various blue and green crumb fabrics for rose backgrounds, and corner and setting triangles – see Rose blocks, and Corner and setting triangles
- 74 x 63in (188 x 160cm) of backing fabric
- ½yd (50cm) of binding fabric
- 74 x 63in (188 x 160cm) of wadding (batting)

Cutting instructions

Sashing fabric
- One hundred and twenty 1½ x 7in sashing strips
- Seventy-one 1½in squares

Binding fabric
- Seven 2½in wide strips across the width of the fabric

Rose blocks

1 For each rose, start with a four-sided to six-sided rose centre piece, no bigger than 2–2½in on any given side.

2 Right sides together, place a 1–2in wide rose strip along one edge of your centre piece.

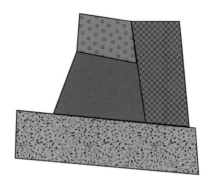

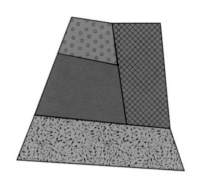

3 Sew in place and trim the excess fabric level with the edge of the centre piece.

4 Continue adding rose strips of the same colourway around your centre piece Log Cabin style until you have completed two rounds.

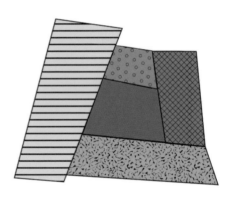

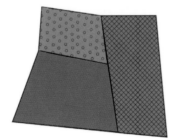

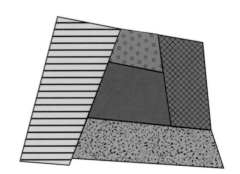

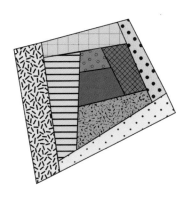

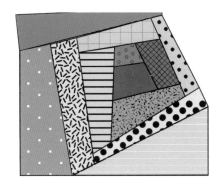

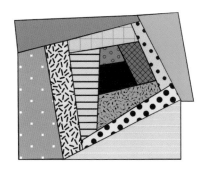

5 Next add rose background crumb 'chunks' to the block, again in Log Cabin style, until you have a unit that can be trimmed to 7in square. Refer to Steps 6 and 7 for background colourways.

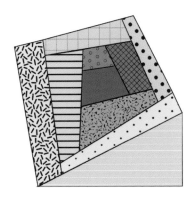

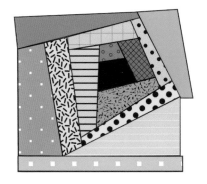

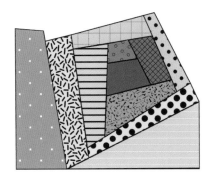

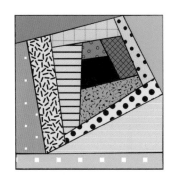

6 Following Steps 1–5, make eleven rose blocks each in pink, purple, red and yellow, with their backgrounds as follows:
- Seven rose blocks with blue backgrounds
- Three rose blocks with green backgrounds
- One rose block with a mixed blue and green background

7 Following Steps 1–5, make six orange rose blocks, with their backgrounds as follows:
- Three rose blocks with blue backgrounds
- Two rose blocks with green backgrounds
- One rose block with a mixed blue and green background

Corner and setting triangles

8 Use blue crumb fabrics to create one 8in made crumb-fabric square. Square up to 7½in square. Cut once on the diagonal.

> TIP **To create made crumb-fabric units such as squares, sew crumb squares and strips together in a Log Cabin and/or Rail Fence fashion until you have a made crumb-fabric piece of the required size. A picture tutorial for this can be found at: www.auntemsquilts.com/blog/fabric-from-scraps**

9 Repeat Step 8 with green crumb fabrics.

10 These are your four corner triangles. Set aside.

11 Use blue crumb fabrics to create three 12in made crumb-fabric squares. Square up to 11¼in square. Cut each square twice on the diagonal.

12 Repeat Step 11 to create two 12in green made crumb-fabric squares. Square up to 11¼in square. Cut each square twice on the diagonal.

13 These are your eighteen setting triangles. (You will have two spare blue triangles.)

Quilt layout

14 Following On-point settings (see General Techniques, Piecing), and referring to the flat shot for colour placements, sew your rose blocks, sashing strips and squares, and corner and setting triangles together. Trim so you have straight edges. Your quilt top is now complete.

Quilting and finishing

15 Make a quilt sandwich of the quilt top, the wadding (batting) and the backing fabric (see General Techniques, Making a quilt sandwich).

16 Quilt as desired. I quilted leaves and vines all over the quilt surface (see General Techniques, Quilting).

17 Square-up and bind to finish (see General Techniques, Squaring-up your quilt and Binding).

UNDER THE SEA

Create an underwater party of sea creatures,
swimming in an ocean of crumb scraps.

Approximate size: 59 x 51in (150 x 130cm)

MATERIALS

- Various fabrics – see each block's instructions for details
- 67 x 59in (170 x 150cm) of backing fabric
- ½yd (50cm) of binding fabric
- 67 x 59in (170 x 150cm) of wadding (batting)

Cutting instructions

Various fabrics
- See each block's instructions for details

Binding fabric
- Six 2½in wide strips across the width of the fabric

Basic units

Half-square triangles (HSTs)

1 On the wrong side of one of a pair of squares, draw a diagonal line from corner to corner.

2 Place the squares right sides together with the marked square on top. Sew ¼in either side of drawn line. Cut through both layers on the marked line; open the units out and press. Keeping the 45-degree line of your ruler aligned with the diagonal seam, trim to size. You will now have two identical HSTs.

Sew-and-flip corners

3 On the wrong side of the small square draw a diagonal line from corner to corner. Place on the corner of other (larger) piece as instructed, right sides together and with the drawn line running from outer edge to outer edge of the larger piece. Sew on the drawn line.

4 Press open and then trim the seam allowance.

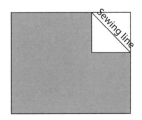

Flying geese units

5 Sew-and-flip a square to one side of a rectangle (the rectangle will be the same height as the square), sewing from the top edge to the bottom corner. Repeat on the other side of the rectangle to complete one flying goose unit.

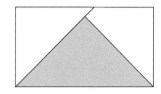

Cutting instructions are height x width of how the pieces appear in the quilt. Refer to the relevant diagram when constructing each block.

Whale

Cutting instructions

SEA FABRICS
- One 1½ x 5½in rectangle
- Six 2½in squares
- One 2½ x 8½in rectangle
- One 4½ x 2½in rectangle
- One 5in square

WHALE FABRICS
- Two 2½ x 4½in rectangles
- One 3½ x 5½in rectangle
- One 4½ x 5½in rectangle
- One 4½ x 6½in rectangle
- One 5in square
- One 8½ x 3½in rectangle

Sewing

6 Use the 5in sea and 5in whale squares to make two HSTs. Trim to 4½in square.

7 Sew-and-flip a 2½in sea square to the upper right-hand corner of the 4½ x 5½in whale rectangle.

8 Sew-and-flip a 2½in sea square to the bottom right-hand corner of the 3½ x 5½in whale rectangle.

9 Sew the 1½ x 5½in sea rectangle between them.

10 Sew-and-flip a 2½in sea square to the right-hand side of a 2½ x 4½in whale rectangle, sewing from the top left to the bottom right corner. Then sew-and-flip a 2½in sea square to the left-hand side, sewing from the bottom right to the top left corner.

11 Mirror the process described in Step 10 with the remaining 2½in sea squares and 2½ x 4½in whale rectangle.

12 Join these pieces to create the V-shaped whale's tail.

13 Sew the 2½ x 8½in sea rectangle to the top of the tail.

14 Sew one of the HSTs to the right-hand side of this unit.

15 Sew the remaining HST between the 4½ x 2½in sea rectangle and the 4½ x 6½in whale rectangle.

16 Sew this to the bottom of the unit made in Step 14.

17 Sew the 8½ x 3½in whale rectangle between the units made in Steps 9 and 16. The whale block should measure 8½ x 20½in.

Striped fish

Cutting instructions
SEA FABRICS
- Six 1½in squares

HEAD AND TAIL FABRIC
- Three 2½ x 1½in rectangles

ALTERNATE FABRIC
- Two 2½ x 1½in rectangles

Sewing
18 Use four 1½in sea squares and two 2½ x 1½in head and tail rectangles to make two flying geese units.

19 Use two 1½in sea squares and one 2½ x 1½in alternate rectangle to make one flying goose unit.

20 Sew the flying geese units and the remaining 2½ x 1½in head and tail and alternate rectangles together as shown. The striped fish should measure 2½ x 5½in.

21 Make a total of three striped fish.

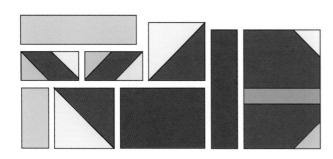

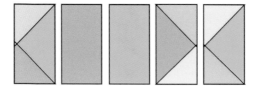

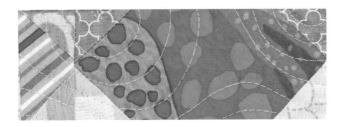

Skinny fish

Cutting instructions

SEA FABRICS
- Six 1½in squares

BODY FABRIC
- One 2½ x 5½in rectangle

TAIL FABRIC
- One 2½ x 1½in rectangle

Sewing

22 Sew-and-flip a 1½in sea square to each corner of the 2½ x 5½in body rectangle.

23 Use two 1½in sea squares and the 2½ x 1½in tail rectangle to make one flying goose unit.

24 Sew the body and tail units together as shown. The skinny fish should measure 2½ x 6½in.

25 Make a total of seven skinny fish.

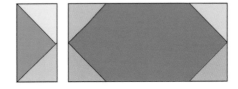

3D fish

Cutting instructions

SEA FABRICS
- Four 1½in squares
- Two 3in squares, each cut once on the diagonal

FISH FABRIC
- One 3¾in square, cut once on the diagonal

FIN AND TAIL FABRIC
- Two 2½ x 1½in rectangles
- One 3in square

Sewing

26 Press the 3in fin square in half on the diagonal, wrong sides together. Press on the diagonal the other way to create a prairie point.

27 Find the centre of the long (cut) sides of one fish triangle. Centre the prairie point along this edge on the right side. Right sides together, place the remaining fish triangle on top. Sew together. Open up. Press the seam upwards and the prairie point downwards. Sew a sea triangle to each corner to complete the body unit.

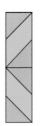

28 Use the 1½in sea squares and the 2½ x 1½in tail rectangles to create the tail (see Steps 10–12).

29 Sew the body unit and tail together. The 3D fish should measure 4½ x 5½in.

30 Make a total of three 3D fish.

Winged fish

Cutting instructions
SEA FABRICS
- Two 1½in squares
- Two 1½ x 2½in rectangles
- One 2in square
- One 3in square
- Two 4in squares, each cut once on the diagonal

FISH FABRIC
- One 2½in square

FIN AND TAIL FABRIC
- One 2in square
- One 3in square

Sewing
31 Use the 2in sea and 2in fin squares to make two HSTs. Trim to 1½in square. Sew a 1½in sea square to the left of each HST, joining it to the sea triangle. Sew a 1½ x 2½in sea rectangle to the top of each unit.

32 Use the 3in sea and 3in tail squares to make two HSTs. Trim to 2½in square. (You will have one spare HST, so could use this in another fish.)

33 Sew the sea/tail HST to left of one unit made in Step 31. Sew the 2½in fish square to the right of the remaining unit. Sew together to create the fish.

34 Sew a sea triangle to each corner of the fish. The winged fish should measure 6½in square.

35 Make a total of three winged fish.

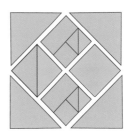

Arrow fish

Cutting instructions
SEA FABRICS
- Two 3in squares
- Two 4in squares, each cut once on the diagonal

FISH FABRIC
- One 3in square
- One 7¼in square, cut twice on the diagonal

Sewing
36 Use one 3in sea square and the 3in fish square to make two HSTs. Trim to 2½in square. Cut the remaining 3in sea square once on the diagonal and sew to one HST as shown (see overleaf). (You will have one spare HST, so could use this in another fish.)

37 Sew a fish triangle to this unit on the diagonal edge as shown. (The remaining fish triangles can be used in the other fish.)

38 Sew a sea triangle to each corner of the fish. The arrow fish should measure 6½in square.

39 Make a total of five arrow fish.

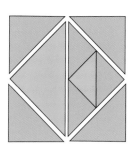

Turtle

Cutting instructions
SEA FABRICS
• Four 1½in squares
• Four 2in squares
• Two 2¼ x 3in rectangles
• Two 2½ x 1½in rectangles
• One 4 x 10in rectangle
• One 4 x 11in rectangle
SHELL FABRIC
• Three 1½ x 30in strips
HEAD, TAIL AND FEET FABRIC
• One 1½ x 2½in rectangle (tail)
• Four 2¾in squares (feet)
• One 3in square (head)

Sewing
40 Sew the 1½ x 30in shell strips into a strip set (see General Techniques, Piecing, Strip piecing). Subcut into sixteen Turtle templates – two sets of eight identical templates. Arrange eight identical templates into an octagon. Sew into pairs and then fours, then sew the two halves together to complete the shell. (The remaining templates can be used for another turtle.)

41 Sew-and-flip a 2in sea square onto opposite corners of a 2¾in feet square. Cut once on the diagonal as shown to make two feet. Repeat.

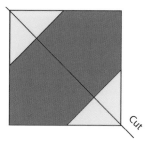

42 Sew a foot to each corner of the shell as shown.

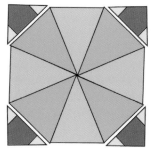

43 Sew-and-flip a 1½in sea square to the top corners of the 3in head square. Sew a 2¼ x 3in sea rectangle to each side as shown to complete the head unit.

44 Use two 1½in sea squares and the 2½ x 1½in tail rectangle to make one flying goose unit. Sew a 2½ x 1½in sea rectangle to each side as shown to complete the tail unit.

45 Sew the head unit and tail unit to opposite sides of the shell as shown to complete the turtle unit.

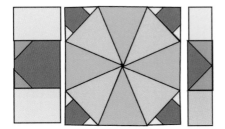

46 Take the 4 x 11in sea rectangle. Place it right side up and cut it on the diagonal as shown. Cut at least ¾in away from the corners.

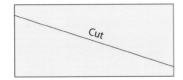

47 Sew these pieces to the sides of the turtle unit as shown. Make sure you join the cut diagonal edges to the turtle unit. Straighten up the top and bottom edges level with the turtle unit as shown.

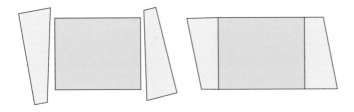

48 Take the 4 x 10in sea rectangle and cut it on the diagonal as described in Step 46. Sew these pieces to the top and bottom of the turtle unit as shown, again making sure you join the cut diagonal edges to the turtle unit. Square up your turtle block.

49 Add sea strips to sides of your turtle block so it measures 11½ x 13½in.

50 Make a total of two turtle blocks.

Coral

Cutting instructions

SEA FABRICS
- One 16½ x 15½in rectangle
- One 16½ x 12½in rectangle
- Scraps (strips or crumbs) for bringing the blocks up to size (see Step 53)

CORAL FABRIC
- A variety of 1½in wide strips

Sewing

51 For each sea fabric rectangle, as shown, make an angled vertical cut near the centre for the trunks of your coral, and then make additional angled horizontal cuts for the branches.

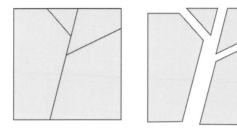

52 In the reverse order that you make the cuts in Step 51, insert 1½in wide coral strips as shown. Straighten up the edges as you add each strip. Square up.

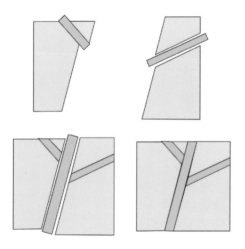

53 Add sea scraps to bring one block up to 16½ x 12½in and the other block up to 16½ x 15½in rectangle.

Jellyfish

Cutting instructions
SEA FABRIC
- One 8½ x 7in made sea-crumb rectangle

JELLYFISH FABRIC AND FUSIBLE WEB
- One Large Jellyfish template
- Three Small Jellyfish templates

MINI RICKRACK
- 1½yds (1.4m)

Sewing

54 Trace the templates onto the paper side of the fusible web and cut out roughly. Following the manufacturer's instructions, fuse to the jellyfish fabric and cut out neatly.

55 Arrange the jellyfish pieces onto the made sea-crumb rectangle. Cut the rickrack into five similar (not identical) lengths for the tentacles. Position a tentacle in the centre of each small template and where the templates meet, placing the top end of the rickrack underneath the jellyfish. Fuse in place as per the manufacturer's instructions.

56 Stitch the rickrack tentacles down. Blanket stitch around the jellyfish pieces. The jellyfish should measure 8½ x 7in.

57 Make a total of three jellyfish blocks.

Quilt layout

Follow the layout diagram when constructing the quilt top. The sizes on the diagram are given height x width and are the unfinished sizes (in inches).

ABBREVIATIONS
- **Stp fish:** Striped fish
- **Sk fish:** Skinny fish

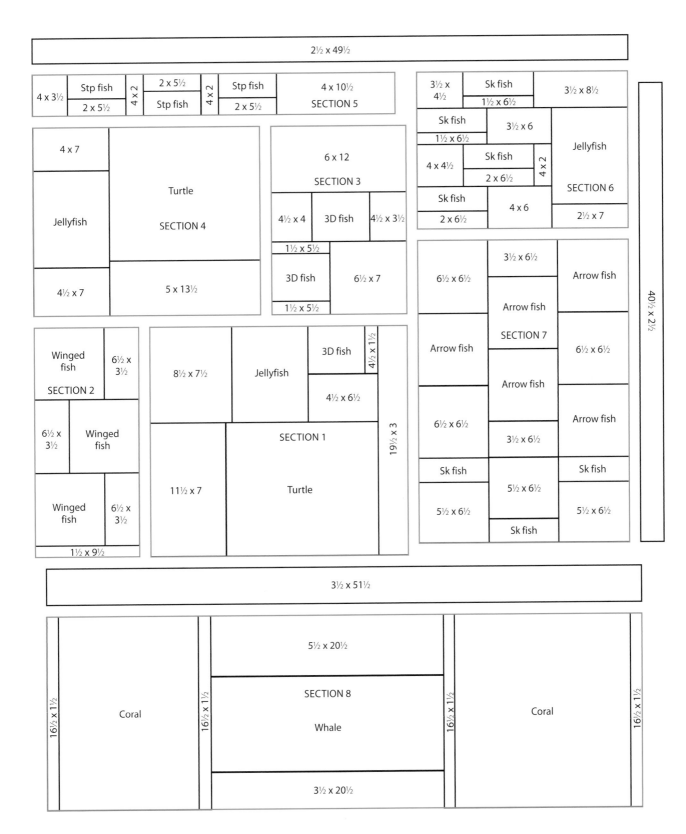

58 You will need to create several made sea-crumb units for the quilt top. Refer to the layout diagram for the sizes required. You may prefer to cut smaller pieces from a single scrap of sea fabric.

TIP **To create made sea-crumb units, sew sea crumb squares and strips together in a Log Cabin and/or Rail Fence fashion until you have a made sea-crumb piece of the required size. A picture tutorial for this can be found at: www.auntemsquilts.com/blog/fabric-from-scraps**

59 Section 1:
- Sew an 11½ x 7in made-fabric rectangle to the left side of a turtle block and set aside
- Sew a 4½ x 1½in made-fabric rectangle to the right side of a 3D fish
- Sew a 4½ x 6½in made-fabric rectangle beneath this unit
- Sew a jellyfish block to the left of this unit
- Sew an 8½ x 7½in made-fabric rectangle to the left of this unit
- Sew this unit to the top of the turtle unit
- Sew a 19½ x 3in made-fabric rectangle to the right side of this unit

60 Construct Sections 2–8, building them up in a similar manner as for Section 1.

61 Joining the sections:
- Sew Section 1 to the right of Section 2
- Sew Section 3 to the right of Section 4
- Sew Section 3/4 to the top of Section 1/2
- Sew Section 5 to the top of this unit
- Sew Section 6 to the top of Section 7
- Sew Section 6/7 to the previous unit
- Sew a 2½ x 49½in made-fabric strip to the top of this unit
- Sew a 40½ x 2½in made-fabric strip to the right of this unit
- Sew a 3½ x 51½in made-fabric strip to the bottom of this unit
- Sew Section 8 to the bottom of this unit

62 Your quilt top is now complete.

Quilting and finishing

63 Make a quilt sandwich of the quilt top, the wadding (batting) and the backing fabric (see General Techniques, Making a quilt sandwich).

64 Quilt as desired. I quilted using alternating rows of swirling waves and echoing waving lines (see General Techniques, Quilting).

65 Square-up and bind to finish (see General Techniques, Squaring-up your quilt and Binding).

NIGHT SKY

Dig deep in your stash for gorgeous inky blues so the bright happy stars will simply sparkle in your scrappy night-time sky.

Approximate size: 59 x 49in (150 x 125cm)

MATERIALS

- Background fabrics – scraps and crumbs totalling approximately 4yds (3.7m)
- Star fabrics – scraps totalling approximately 1yd (1m)
- 67 x 57in (170 x 145cm) of backing fabric
- ½yd (50cm) of binding fabric
- 67 x 57in (170 x 145cm) of wadding (batting)

Cutting instructions

Background fabrics
- See instructions for details

Star fabrics
- See instructions for details

Binding fabric
- Six 2½in wide strips across the width of the fabric

Maverick Stars

For small stars, use 1½in squares. For large stars, use 2½in squares.

Cutting instructions
BACKGROUND FABRICS
- Eight squares

STAR FABRICS
- One square
- Various scraps for star points

Sewing
1 Take one background square and place a star scrap along it diagonally as shown. Make sure the star scrap will cover the bottom left corner of the square once it is sewn in place and flipped open.

2 Sew ¼in in from the lower edge of the scrap. Flip open and press.

3 Trim level with the edges of the background square. If you wish, trim the seam allowance.

4 Repeat for the bottom right corner of the square to complete one star point.

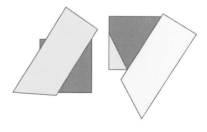

5 Repeat Steps 1–4 to make a total of four star points.

TIP **When making the star points, placing the star scraps at different angles will add variety to your Maverick Stars.**

6 Arrange the star points, the remaining background squares and the star square as shown. Sew into rows and then join the rows to complete a Maverick Star block.

7 Make a total of five large Maverick Star blocks, which should measure 6½in square. Make a total of nineteen small Maverick Star blocks, which should measure 3½in square.

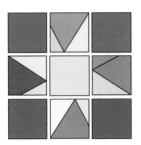

Large Friendship Stars

Cutting instructions

BACKGROUND FABRICS
- Four 2½in squares
- Two 3in squares

STAR FABRICS
- One 2½in square
- Two 3in squares

Sewing

8 On the wrong side of a 3in star square, draw a diagonal line from corner to corner.

9 Right sides together, place the star square on top of a 3in background square. Sew ¼in either side of drawn line.

10 Cut through both layers on the marked line; open the units out and press. Keeping the 45-degree line of your ruler aligned with the diagonal seam, trim to 2½in square. You will now have two identical half-square triangles (HSTs).

11 Make a total of four HSTs.

12 Arrange the HSTs and the 2½in background and star squares as shown. Sew into rows and then join the rows to complete a large Friendship Star. This should measure 6½in square.

13 Create two 5in made background-crumb squares. Cut each once on the diagonal to give four triangles. Sew the long (cut) edges of a triangle to each side of the large Friendship Star. Square up to 8½in square.

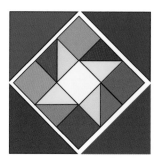

14 Make a total of two large Friendship Star blocks.

Small Friendship Stars

Cutting instructions
BACKGROUND FABRICS
- Four 2in squares
- Two 2½in squares

STAR FABRICS
- One 2in square
- Two 2½in squares

Sewing

15 Follow Steps 8–12 to make a small Friendship Star. (Use the 2½in squares to make the HSTs.) This should measure 5in square.

16 Create two 4¼in made background-crumb squares. Cut each once on the diagonal to give four triangles. Sew the long (cut) edges of a triangle to each side of the Friendship Star. Square up to 7½in square.

17 Make a total of three small Friendship Star blocks.

Elongated Stars

Cutting instructions
BACKGROUND FABRICS
- Four 3¼in squares – I created some of mine from made background-crumb squares
- Eight 2 x 4½in rectangles

STAR FABRICS
- One 3in square
- Eight 2 x 4½in rectangles

Sewing

18 Place a background rectangle on top of a star rectangle, both facing right side up. Cut on the diagonal from top left to bottom right.

19 Sew the created background triangles to the created star triangles as shown (see overleaf).

20 Open out and press. Square up to 3¼ x 1¾in. This will give you two Unit A half-rectangle triangles.

21 Repeat Steps 18–20 to make a total of eight Unit A half-rectangle triangles.

22 Place a background rectangle on top of a star rectangle, both facing right side up. Cut on the diagonal from top right to bottom left.

23 Sew the created background triangles to the created star triangles as before. Open out and press. Square up to 3¼ x 1¾in. This will give you two Unit B half-rectangle triangles.

24 Repeat Steps 22 and 23 to make a total of eight Unit B half-rectangle triangles.

25 Sew a Unit A half-rectangle triangle to a Unit B half-rectangle triangle as shown to create a star point. Trim to 3¼ x 3in.

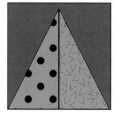

TIP **When making the star points, don't worry if the points aren't perfect. As most of the stars in this project are wonky anyway, this will just add to the character of your quilt!**

26 Repeat Step 25 to make a total of four star points. (You will have eight Unit A and eight Unit B half-rectangle triangles spare, which can be used in other Elongated Star blocks.)

27 Arrange the star points, the 3in star square and the 3¼in background squares as shown. Sew into rows and then join the rows to complete an Elongated Star block. This should measure 8½in.

28 Make a total of five Elongated Star blocks.

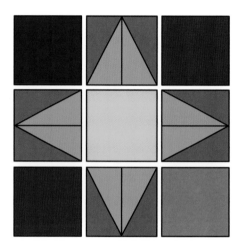

Quilt layout

29 You will need to create several made background-crumb units for the quilt top. Refer to the layout diagram for the sizes required. You may prefer to cut smaller pieces from a single scrap of background fabric.

Follow the layout diagram when constructing the quilt top. The sizes on the diagram are given height x width and are the unfinished sizes (in inches).

ABBREVIATIONS
- **Large FS:** Large Friendship Star
- **Small FS:** Small Friendship Star
- **Large MS:** Large Maverick Star
- **SMS:** Small Maverick Star

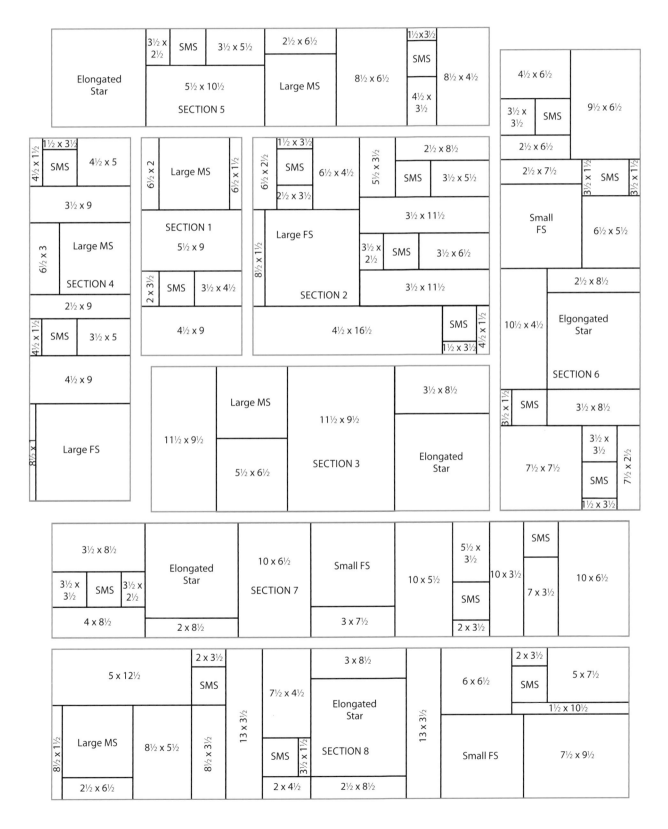

TIP **To create made background-crumb units, sew background crumb squares and strips together in a Log Cabin and/or Rail Fence fashion until you have a made background-crumb piece of the required size. A picture tutorial for this can be found at: www.auntemsquilts.com/blog/fabric-from-scraps**

30 Section 1:
- Sew a 6½ x 2in made-fabric rectangle to the left side of a large Maverick Star block
- Sew a 6½ x 1½in made-fabric rectangle to the right side of the star
- Sew a 3½ x 2in made-fabric rectangle to the left side of a small Maverick Star block
- Sew a 3½ x 4½in made-fabric rectangle to the right side of the star
- Sew a 5½ x 9in made-fabric rectangle between the large and small Maverick Star units
- Sew a 4½ x 9in made-fabric rectangle beneath the small Maverick Star unit

31 Construct Sections 2–8, building them up in a similar manner as for Section 1.

32 Joining the sections:
- Sew Section 1 to the left of Section 2
- Sew Section 3 beneath this unit
- Sew Section 4 to the left of this unit
- Sew Section 5 to the top of this unit
- Sew Section 6 to the right of this unit
- Sew Section 7 beneath this unit
- Sew Section 8 beneath this unit

33 Your quilt top is now complete.

Quilting and finishing

34 Make a quilt sandwich of the quilt top, the wadding (batting) and the backing fabric (see General Techniques, Making a quilt sandwich).

35 Quilt as desired. I quilted continuous strings of stars, with the stars separated by a wavy organic line a few inches long. Alternate strings of stars are offset to create the effect of nested stars across the quilt's surface (see General Techniques, Quilting).

36 Square-up and bind to finish (see General Techniques, Squaring-up your quilt and Binding).

REMEMBERING IDA

My great-grandmother Ida Mabel Miller was a widow raising children during the Great Depression. I am fortunate enough to have some of her quilts and I created this one to feature the traditional blocks she liked to use.

Approximate size: 72 x 60in (183 x 153cm)

MATERIALS

- Various background made crumb fabric – see each unit's instructions
- Various print made crumb fabric – see each unit's instructions
- 80 x 68in (203 x 173cm) of backing fabric
- ⅝yd (60cm) of binding fabric
- 80 x 68in (203 x 173cm) of wadding (batting)

TIP For small background and print pieces, you may find it easier to use scraps (crumb fabric) rather than made crumb fabric. Using lots of different fabrics will give the made crumb-fabric effect without having to deal with lots of seams.

TIP For some units, using a flying geese ruler is an efficient way to cut out pieces, so we have given this as an alternative where appropriate. For how to use a flying geese ruler, see General Techniques, Cutting, Flying geese ruler.

Cutting instructions

Various background made crumb fabric
- See each block's instructions for details

Various print made crumb fabric
- See each block's instructions for details

Binding fabric
- Seven 2½in wide strips across the width of the fabric

Basic units

Half-square triangles (HSTs)

1 On the wrong side of one of a pair of squares, draw a diagonal line from corner to corner.

2 Place the squares right sides together with the marked square on top. Sew ¼in either side of drawn line. Cut through both layers on the marked line; open the units out and press. Keeping the 45-degree line of your ruler aligned with the diagonal seam, trim to size. You will now have two identical HSTs.

Sew-and-flip corners

3 On the wrong side of the small square draw a diagonal line from corner to corner. Place on the corner of the other (larger) piece as instructed, right sides together and with the drawn line running from outer edge to outer edge of the larger piece. Sew on the drawn line.

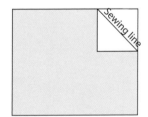

TIP When making your blocks, save larger pieces of leftover crumb fabrics as you may be able to use these in other blocks. Waste not, want not!

4 Press open and then trim the seam allowance.

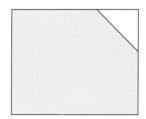

Flying geese units

5 Sew-and-flip a square to one side of a rectangle (the rectangle will be the same height as the square), sewing from top edge to the bottom corner. Repeat on the other side of the rectangle to complete one flying goose unit.

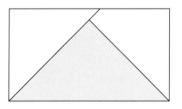

Basket block

Cutting instructions
BACKGROUND CRUMB FABRICS

- One 9in square, cut once on the diagonal
- One 5in square, cut once on the diagonal
- Two 2½ x 6½in rectangles

PRINT CRUMB FABRICS
- One 9in square, cut once on the diagonal
- One 3in square, cut once on the diagonal or from a 2½in wide strip use a flying geese ruler to cut two HSTs

STANDARD RICKRACK
- One 10½in length

Sewing

6 Take one 9in background triangle and place it right side up. Take the rickrack and arrange it on top in the shape of a basket handle; make sure it is centred and that the raw ends of the rickrack are aligned with the raw edges of the diagonal edge of the triangle. Pin or glue the handle in place and then sew to secure. (One 9in background triangle will be spare and could be used in another block.)

7 Take one 9in print triangle and place it right sides together with the background/handle triangle. Sew together on the diagonal edge. The raw ends of the rickrack will be trapped in the seam. (One 9in print triangle will be spare and could be used in another block.)

8 Keeping the handle centred and the 45-degree line of your ruler aligned with the diagonal seam, trim to 8½in square.

9 As shown, sew a 3in print triangle to the right-hand end of one 2½ x 6½in background rectangle. Sew the remaining 3in print triangle to the left-hand end of the other 2½ x 6½in background rectangle.

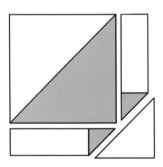

TIP **When sewing the 3in print triangles to the ends of the 2½ x 6½in background rectangles, align one straight edge of the triangle with the long edge of the rectangle, and the other straight edge with the short edge of the rectangle (the triangle will overhang at the other end of the rectangle's short edge).**

10 As shown, sew one rectangle/triangle unit to the bottom (a print edge) of the unit made in Step 8, and sew the other rectangle/triangle unit to the right-hand side (a print edge).

11 As shown, sew a 5in background triangle to the bottom right-hand corner of the unit made in Step 10. (One 5in background triangle will be spare and could be used in another block.)

12 Square up to 10½in square. This completes one basket block.

13 Make a total of six basket blocks.

TIP **If you have one, you will find a design wall useful for keeping track of your blocks and units, arranging them as shown in the layout diagram as you go. If you don't have a design wall, a large sheet pinned to a curtain works well as alternative, or you could hang a large piece of wadding on the wall.**

Shoo Fly block

Cutting instructions
BACKGROUND CRUMB FABRICS
- Two 4in squares or from a 3½in wide strip use a flying geese ruler to cut four HSTs
- Four 3½ x 6½in rectangles

PRINT CRUMB FABRICS
- One 6½in square
- Two 4in squares or from a 3½in wide strip use a flying geese ruler to cut four HSTs

Sewing

14 Use the 4in background and 4in print squares to make four HSTs. Trim to 3½in square.

15 Arrange the 3½ x 6½in background rectangles, the 6½in print square and the HSTs as shown (see overleaf).

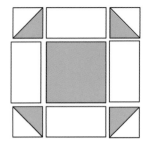

22 Sew the remaining 2 x 11in rectangle to the left-hand side and the 2 x 12½in rectangle to the top of the nine-patch.

23 Square up to 12½in square. This completes one framed nine-patch block.

24 Make a total of two framed nine-patch blocks.

16 Sew into rows and then sew the rows together.

17 Square up to 12½in square. This completes one Shoo Fly block.

18 Make a total of two Shoo Fly blocks.

Framed nine-patch block

Cutting instructions
BACKGROUND CRUMB FABRICS
- Four 3½in squares
- One 2 x 9½in rectangle
- Two 2 x 11in rectangles
- One 2 x 12½in rectangle

PRINT CRUMB FABRICS
- Five 3½in squares

Sewing
19 Alternating them, arrange the four 3½in background squares and the five 3½in print squares into a nine-patch layout (three rows of three).

20 Sew into rows and then sew the rows together.

21 Sew the 2 x 9½in background rectangle to the right-hand side of the nine-patch and a 2 x 11in rectangle to the bottom.

Framed heart block

Cutting instructions
BACKGROUND CRUMB FABRICS
- One 5in square
- Four 2½in squares
- Two 2½ x 8½in rectangles
- Two 2½ x 12½in rectangles

PRINT CRUMB FABRICS
- One 5in square
- Two 4½in squares

Sewing
25 Sew-and-flip a 2½in background square to the top corners only of the 4½in print squares.

26 Use the 5in background and 5in print squares to make two HSTs. Trim to 4½in square.

27 Arrange the sew-and-flip units and the HSTs as shown.

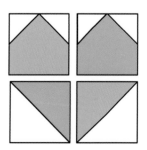

28 Sew into rows and then sew the rows together.

29 Sew a 2½ x 8½in background rectangle to the top and bottom of the heart.

30 Sew a 2½ x 12½in background rectangle to each side of the heart.

31 Square up to 12½in square. This completes the framed heart block.

Pinwheel star block

Cutting instructions
BACKGROUND CRUMB FABRICS
- Six 7½in squares or from a 6½in wide strip use a flying geese ruler to cut twelve HSTs
- Four 6½in squares

PRINT CRUMB FABRICS
- Six 7½in squares or from a 6½in wide strip use a flying geese ruler to cut twelve HSTs

Sewing
32 Use the 7½in background and 7½in print squares to make twelve HSTs. Trim to 6½in square.

33 Arrange four of the HSTs into two rows of two, making sure you orientate them as shown. Sew into rows and then sew the rows together to make the pinwheel centre.

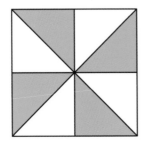

34 Take two of the remaining HSTs and sew together as shown. Repeat to make four of these units.

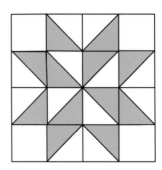

35 Sew a unit made in Step 34 to each side of the pinwheel centre as shown.

36 Sew a 6½in background square to each end of the remaining units made in Step 34. Sew these to the top and bottom of the pinwheel centre.

37 Square up to 24½in square. This completes the pinwheel star block

Flying geese row

Cutting instructions
BACKGROUND CRUMB FABRICS
- Sixteen 3½in squares or from a 3½in wide strip use a flying geese ruler to cut sixteen HSTs

PRINT CRUMB FABRICS
- Eight 3½ x 6½in rectangles or from a 3½in wide strip use a flying geese ruler to cut eight quarter-square triangles (QSTs)

Sewing
38 Use two 3½in background squares and one 3½ x 6½in print rectangle to make one flying goose unit.

39 Make a total of eight flying geese units.

40 Sew the units into a row on their 6½in edges, making sure all the geese are flying in the same direction. The row should measure 3½ x 24½in.

O blocks

Cutting instructions
BACKGROUND CRUMB FABRICS
- Eight 3½in squares

PRINT CRUMB FABRICS
- Four 6½in squares

Sewing
41 Sew-and-flip a 3½in background square to two opposite corners of a 6½in print square. Sew the pairs of triangles trimmed from each corner together on their diagonal edges to give you two HSTs. Save these for the Pinwheel units.

42 Make a total of four sew-and-flip units.

43 Arrange the sew-and-flip units as shown. Sew into rows and then sew the rows together.

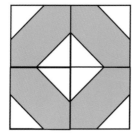

44 Square up to 12½in square. This completes one O block.

45 Make a total of two O blocks. You will have sixteen saved HSTs, which will be enough for your Pinwheel units.

Pinwheel units

Cutting instructions
BACKGROUND CRUMB FABRICS
- Two 6½in squares
- Four 3¾in squares or the HSTs saved from the O blocks
- Two 2 x 6½in rectangles
- Two 2 x 5in rectangles

PRINT CRUMB FABRICS
- Four 3¾in squares or the HSTs saved from the O blocks

Sewing
46 Use the 3¾in background and 3¾in print squares to make eight HSTs. Trim to 2¾in square.

47 Arrange four of the HSTs into two rows of two, making sure you orientate them as shown. Sew into rows and then sew the rows together. This completes one pinwheel block.

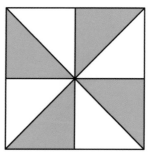

48 Make a total of two pinwheel blocks.

49 Sew a 2 x 5in background rectangle to the bottom edge of each pinwheel block. Sew a 2 x 6½in background rectangle to an adjacent side of each pinwheel block. This completes two half-framed pinwheel blocks.

50 Referring to the layout diagram, arrange the 6½in background squares and the half-framed pinwheel blocks (making sure you orientate them as shown) into two rows of two. Sew into rows and then sew the rows together.

51 Square up to 12½in square. This completes one pinwheel unit.

52 Make a total of two pinwheel units.

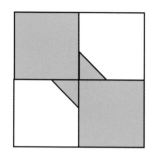

55 Square up to 6½in square. This completes one Bow Tie block.

56 Make a total of four Bow Tie blocks.

57 Sew the blocks into a row, making sure they are all orientated in the same direction. The row should measure 6½ x 24½in.

Bow Tie row

Cutting instructions
BACKGROUND CRUMB FABRICS
• Two 3½in squares
PRINT CRUMB FABRICS
• Two 3½in squares
• Two 1½in squares

Sewing
53 Sew-and-flip a 1½in print square to one corner only of each 3½in background square.

54 Arrange the 3½in print squares and 3½in sew-and-flip squares into two rows of two as shown. Sew into rows and then sew the rows together.

Chequerboard row

Cutting instructions
BACKGROUND CRUMB FABRICS
• Twelve 2½in squares
PRINT CRUMB FABRICS
• Twelve 2½in squares

Sewing
58 Sew a 2½in background square to a 2½in print square to make a pair of squares.

59 Make a total of twelve pairs of squares.

60 Referring to the layout diagram, arrange the pairs of squares into two rows of six pairs each, making sure the background and print squares alternate.

61 Sew the pairs of squares into rows and then sew the rows together.

62 This completes the chequerboard row. It should measure 4½ x 24½in.

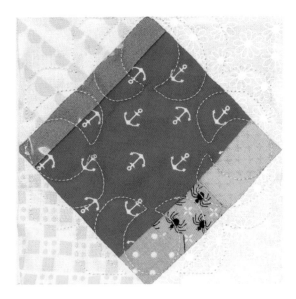

Square-in-a-square row

Cutting instructions

BACKGROUND CRUMB FABRICS
• Two 2⅞in squares, each cut once on the diagonal

PRINT CRUMB FABRICS
• One 3⅜in square

Sewing

63 Sew a 2⅞in background triangle to each side of the 3⅜in print square as shown.

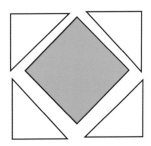

64 Keeping the unit centred, trim to 4½in square. This completes one square-in-a-square unit.

65 Make a total of nine square-in-a-square units.

66 Sew the units into a vertical row. The row should measure 36½ x 4½in.

Houses unit

Cutting instructions

BACKGROUND CRUMB FABRICS
• Eight 2in squares or from a 2in wide strip use a flying geese ruler to cut eight HSTs
• Four 2 x 6½in rectangles
• Eight 2 x 5in rectangles

PRINT CRUMB FABRICS
• Four 3½in squares
• Four 2 x 3½in rectangles or from a 2in wide strip use a flying geese ruler to cut four QSTs

Sewing

67 Use two 2in background squares and one 2 x 3½in print rectangle to make one flying goose unit.

68 Sew the flying goose unit to the top of a 3½in print square, with the print edge of the goose next to the square, to make one house.

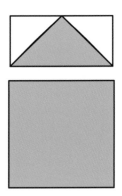

69 Sew a 2 x 5in background rectangle to each side of the house.

70 Sew a 2 x 6½in background rectangle to the top of the house to complete one house block.

71 Make a total of four house blocks.

72 Referring to the layout diagram, arrange the house blocks into two rows of two. Sew into rows and then sew the rows together.

73 This completes the houses unit. It should measure 12½in square.

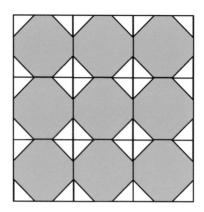

Snowball unit

Cutting instructions
BACKGROUND CRUMB FABRICS
- Thirty-six 1½in squares
- Two 2 x 12½in rectangles
- Two 2 x 9½in rectangles

PRINT CRUMB FABRICS
- Nine 3½in squares

Sewing
74 Sew-and-flip a 1½in background square to each corner of a 3½in print square to make one snowball block.

75 Make a total of nine snowball blocks.

76 Arrange the snowball blocks into a nine-patch layout (three rows of three) as shown. Sew into rows and then sew the rows together.

77 Sew a 2 x 9½in background rectangle to the top and bottom of the snowball nine-patch.

78 Sew a 2 x 12½in background rectangle to each side of the snowball nine-patch.

79 Square up to 12½in square. This completes the snowball unit.

Hourglass star block

Cutting instructions
BACKGROUND CRUMB FABRICS
- Two 5¼in squares, each cut twice on the diagonal or from a 2½in wide strip use a flying geese ruler to cut four QSTs
- Four 4½in squares

PRINT CRUMB FABRICS
- Two 5¼in squares, each cut twice on the diagonal or from a 2½in wide strip use a flying geese ruler to cut four QSTs
- One 4½in square

Sewing

80 Arrange two 5¼in background triangles with two 5¼in print triangles as shown.

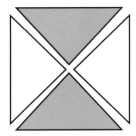

81 Sew together on the diagonal edges to make a QST.

82 Keeping the QST centred, trim to 4½in square.

83 Make a total of four QSTs.

84 Arrange the 4½in background squares, the 4½in print square and the QSTs as shown.

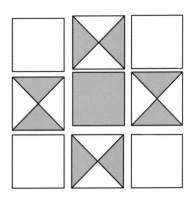

85 Sew into rows and then sew the rows together.

86 Square up to 12½in square. This completes the hourglass star block.

Maverick Star block

Cutting instructions

BACKGROUND CRUMB FABRICS
- Four 2½in squares
- Four 2½ x 4½in rectangles or from a 2½in wide strip use a flying geese ruler to cut four QSTs

PRINT CRUMB FABRICS
- One 4½in square
- Eight 2½in squares or from a 2½in wide strip use a flying geese ruler to cut eight HSTs

Sewing

87 Use two 2½in print squares and one 2½ x 4½in background print rectangle to make one flying goose unit.

88 Make a total of four flying geese units.

89 Arrange the 2½in background squares, the 4½in print square and the flying geese units as shown.

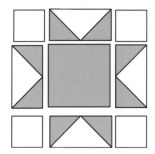

90 Sew into rows and then sew the rows together.

91 Square up to 8½in square. This completes one Maverick Star block.

92 Make a total of four Maverick Star blocks.

Bear Paw unit

Cutting instructions

BACKGROUND CRUMB FABRICS

- Four 3½in squares
- Eight 4in squares or from a 3½in wide strip use a flying geese ruler to cut sixteen HSTs
- Two 2 x 21½in rectangles
- Four 3½ x 9½in rectangles

PRINT CRUMB FABRICS

- Four 6½in squares
- Eight 4in squares or from a 3½in wide strip use a flying geese ruler to cut sixteen HSTs
- One 3½in square

Sewing

93 Use 4in background and 4in print squares to make sixteen HSTs. Trim to 3½in square.

94 Arrange a 3½in background square, a 6½in print square and four HSTs as shown to make the four corners of the Bear Paw block – take care with the placements and orientations. To construct the corners, sew the HSTs into pairs. Sew one pair to the side of the 6½in print square. Sew the 3½in background square to the remaining pair of HSTs and then sew this to the unit to complete a corner

95 Arrange the 3½ x 9½in background rectangles, the 3½in print square and the corners of the Bear Paw block as shown.

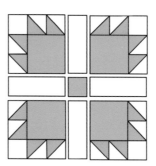

96 Sew into rows and then sew the rows together. This completes the Bear Paw block.

97 Sew a 2 x 21½in background rectangle to each side of the Bear Paw block.

98 This completes the Bear Paw unit. It should measure 21½ x 24½in.

Quilt layout

Follow the layout diagram when constructing the quilt top.

Cutting instructions
BACKGROUND CRUMB FABRICS
- Four 1½ x 8½in rectangles
- One 1½ x 24½in rectangle
- One 2½ x 36½in rectangle

99 Section 1:
- Sew the basket blocks into a row, making sure they are all facing in the same direction

100 Section 2:
- Sew a framed nine-patch block to the top and bottom of the framed heart block
- Sew a Shoo Fly block to the top and bottom of this unit

101 Section 3:
- Sew the flying geese row to the bottom of the pinwheel star block – my geese are flying towards the right
- Arrange the O blocks and pinwheel units into two rows of two as shown. Sew into rows and then sew the rows together.
- Sew the Bow Tie row to the bottom of the O block/pinwheel unit
- Sew the pinwheel star/flying geese to the top of this unit

102 Section 2/3:
- Sew Section 2 to the right-hand side of Section 3
- Sew the 2½ x 36½in background rectangle to the top of this unit

103 Section 4:
- Sew the houses unit to the top of the snowball unit
- Sew the hourglass star block to the bottom of this unit
- Sew the square-in-a-square row to the right-hand side of this unit
- Sew the Maverick Star blocks into a vertical row with a 1½ x 8½in background rectangle between them and a 1½ x 8½in background rectangle at the bottom of the row
- Sew this to the left-hand side of the previous unit
- Sew the chequerboard row to the top of this unit

104 Section 5:
- Sew the 1½ x 24½in background rectangle to the top of the Bear Paw unit

105 Section 4/5:
- Sew Section 4 to the top of Section 5

106 Joining the sections:
- Sew Section 2/3 to the right-hand side of Section 4/5
- Sew Section 1 to the top of this unit

107 Your quilt top is now complete.

Quilting and finishing

108 Make a quilt sandwich of the quilt top, the wadding (batting) and the backing fabric (see General Techniques, Making a quilt sandwich).

109 Quilt as desired. Mine was quilted with different motifs in each block so they stood out. If you prefer, you could quilt an allover pattern (see General Techniques, Quilting).

110 Square-up and bind to finish (see General Techniques, Squaring-up your quilt and Binding).

GENERAL TECHNIQUES

While crumb quilting is unique and fun it still incorporates the quilting techniques used to make any quilt. Following these basic principles will ensure the best possible results and that your quilts will be durable, too.

CUTTING

When cutting appliqué pieces a sharp pair of scissors is best. However, rotary cutters are useful for getting an accurate straight line when cutting pieces of fabric.

> SAFETY **Rotary cutters are very sharp. When not in use make sure the blade is covered. When cutting, make sure fingers are away from the blade. With the hand that holds the cutter, keep fingers on the handle away from the blade. With the hand not holding the cutter, keep fingers firmly on the cutting ruler, away from the ruler's edges.**

Squaring-up your fabric

1 Press the fabric to get rid of any creases.

2 Fold the fabric in half across its width, i.e. so selvedge edges meet. Ensure there are no wrinkles – the cut edges may not line up.

3 Place a 6 x 24in ruler on fabric so that the 1in line is on the fold and the 24in edge of the ruler runs along one of the cut edges of the fabric, making sure that the ruler is over a double thickness of fabric.

4 Cut along the edge of the ruler nearest to the cut edges to straighten up the edge.

Cutting crumb fabric

When cutting crumb fabric, start by straightening up one edge. Cut rectangular units as you would a single piece of fabric. Once the piece is cut, it is a good idea to clean up bulk around the edges. Do this by removing any fabric tails, as well as unpicking where there are seams and intersections that would create bulk when adding these pieces to your blocks and units.

Flying geese ruler

A flying geese ruler is an efficient way to cut half-square triangles (HSTs) and quarter-square triangles (QSTs) from crumb fabric.

1 For HSTs, cut a strip of fabric of the width instructed. Line the ruler up with the bottom edge of the strip and cut as shown (see image 1).

2 Flip the ruler, aligning it with the cut just made as shown. Cut across the strip (see image 2).

3 Continue in this way until you have the number of HSTs required.

4 For QSTs, cut a strip of fabric of the width instructed. Place the ruler with its tip aligned with the top edge of the strip and cut along both sides of the ruler as shown (see image 3).

5 Flip the ruler, aligning its tip with the bottom edge of the strip and one side with the cut just made, then cut along the other side of the ruler as shown (see image 4).

6 Continue in this way until you have the number of QSTs required.

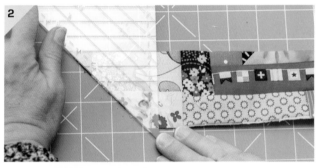

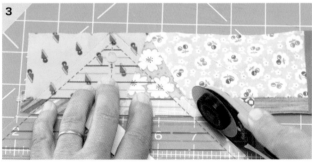

PIECING

Piecing not only creates the look and design of your quilt, but is also a quilt's underlying structure. Using good piecing techniques will ensure you have a beautiful quilt that will last.

Accurate ¼in seams

In quilt-making, a ¼in seam is used when sewing fabric pieces together. Test your ¼in seam by placing two 2¼ x 4in rectangles right sides together and then sew along one 4in edge. Press the seam to one side. Your piece should measure exactly 4in square. If it doesn't, adjust your needle's position or use a line of masking (painter's) tape on your throat plate, adjusting things until you make a 4in square. Doing this will save you a lot of headaches later. Even very slight variations add up as your quilt grows, making it increasingly difficult to fit things together as the quilt progresses.

Stitch length

I like to use a stitch length that gives approximately twelve stitches per inch. On my sewing machine, this is a setting of 2.5, but it will vary from machine to machine, so your setting may be different, so test a few settings before you begin piecing. If your seams come undone at the ends, try a shorter stitch length. If the seam puckers, or the thread looks too loose, before messing with your machine's tension, there are a few things you can try first: change the needle – a nick or flaw in a needle will affect the way it sews; take out the bobbin and make sure there are no threads or lint messing things up; re-thread your machine – I'm amazed how many times this has fixed my problem; make sure you are using high-quality thread, as this too can affect the running of a machine.

Pinning

A pin can be your best friend, helping you to line up seams and points, and to distribute fabric evenly over longer seams. When 'nesting' seams, pin the side of the seam that will reach the needle last, as this allows you to take out the pin as you are sewing without the seam shifting. When joining sections of your quilt where multiple seams will intersect, use a pin at each intersection. But don't worry too much if not everything matches up perfectly. Quilting is meant to be fun and once the quilt is complete the beauty will shine through and a few mismatched seams will only add to the character of your quilt. And most of the time, you'll be the only one that notices anyway.

Chain piecing

Chain piecing is like a mini-assembly line, and is a good way to save time and thread. Once pieces are ready to sew together, you can feed them through your machine one after the other without cutting the thread. Once all the pieces have been sewn, simply clip threads between each unit.

TIP **Before you start chain piecing, make sure your bobbin is full. If it runs out part way through your chain, the chain will fall apart and you will have to go back and re-sew. I've done this far too many times and don't recommend it!**

Strip piecing

This is an easy way to make a set of squares without having to sew each square together individually. Start by sewing strips of the same width together along their long edges, sewing adjacent seams in opposite directions to help prevent 'bowing'. Set the seams (see Pressing seams) and press them all in the same direction.

Lining up gridlines on your ruler with the seam lines (to ensure your strip set will be square), cut segments of the desired width. For squares, cut segments the width of the cut strips you've sewn together.

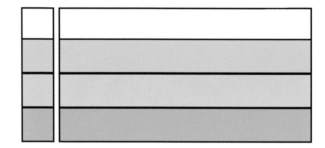

Pressing seams

Generally, seams are pressed towards the darker fabric, but as made crumb fabric contains lots of seams, I prefer to press my seams to the side with the least resistance. Pressing uses the weight of the iron and steam to get your seam to lie flat and remove wrinkles. I like to set the seam first, which just means pressing the seam before the fabric pieces are opened out. Next, I open up the two pieces and press the seam to the side of least resistance. Once again I place the iron down and press – don't move the iron from side to side as this can cause distortion. I like to use steam. When a piece of made crumb fabric is finished, or I've completed a block, I like to give it a spray with starch and press once more.

I know many quilters press seams open, but I feel this weakens the seam and reduces the durability of the quilt. So I only press a seam open if bulk pressing to either side is an issue.

On-point settings

When setting a quilt on-point the rows are sewn together diagonally instead of in straight horizontal rows. Setting triangles are used to make the edges straight, and corner squares are added at each corner. If sashing is being used, it is added just as you would with a straight set quilt, but the sashing strips are sewn as part of the diagonal rows.

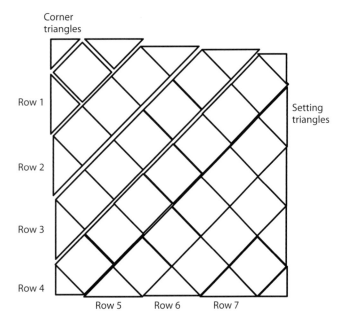

MAKING A QUILT SANDWICH

Making a quilt sandwich, also known as layering or basting, holds the three layers (quilt top, wadding (batting) and backing) of your quilt together to prevent things shifting while you quilt.

There are several basting methods, but I prefer to pin using curved safety pins for quilters. This method is best for machine quilting as it's easy to remove the pins as you work. Quilts can be hand-tacked, but I don't recommend this if you are planning to quilt by machine as the machine's foot can get caught in the tacking stitches. Smaller projects can be spray basted, but this is less successful for larger projects as it's difficult to keep the backing pucker free.

> TIP **For larger quilts, the backing and wadding (batting) should be approximately 4in bigger all around than the quilt top. For smaller makes, like runners and pillows, 2in bigger all around is fine.**

1 Gather your quilt top, wadding, backing, curved safety pins and masking (painter's) tape. Press your quilt top and backing.

2 Place your backing wrong side up on a large, clean, flat surface. I like to put two banquet tables together, but the floor is fine. Smooth out your backing so it is completely flat and without wrinkles, but don't stretch it. Use masking (painter's) tape to hold it in place on whatever surface you are using. Sometimes, I use large binder clips to hold my layers to the banquet tables, folding the edge of the backing over the lip of the table and using the binder clip to hold it in place.

3 Spread the wadding centrally on top of the backing. Gently smooth it out from the centre outwards, being careful not to stretch it.

4 Next, right side up, place your quilt top centrally on top of the wadding. Again, smooth out the wrinkles from the centre outwards, taking care not to stretch or distort it.

5 Using curved safety pins, pin all three layers together in a grid format. Place the pins 4–5in apart all over the quilt's surface.

6 Remove the tape or binder clips and the quilt is ready for quilting.

QUILTING

The quilts in this book were all machine quilted. The smaller ones I did on my domestic machine. My friend, Ruth Davis, quilted the larger ones on her long-arm machine. Hand-quilting is also an option. If you are worried about quilting, there are others who will do it for a fee. I recommend asking to see samples of their work, as this will ensure you like their style and helps to eliminate surprises when you get your quilt back.

If you plan to quilt on your domestic machine, I suggest you sketch out a few plans first. This will give you an idea of how a design will look, and it creates 'muscle memory' for when you begin to quilt for real. I like to take a picture of a section of my quilt and then blow it up in size. I then place clear vinyl or thick plastic over the image and use a dry-erase marker to draw different quilting motifs until I hit on one I like.

When quilting on a domestic machine, it's a good idea to have a table behind you and to the left of your machine, as this will help to support your quilt and take some of the weight, making it easier to move the quilt around as you are quilting. I like to start in the centre of my quilt and work my way outwards. This helps to prevent puckers in the middle of the quilt – and it gets the hardest part to quilt out of the way first. As you get closer to the edges, there is less fabric bunched up against your machine, so it's easier to manoeuvre your quilt.

Quilting design options

Choosing a quilt design can be overwhelming. The following suggestions should help to get your creative juices flowing – use them as a starting point and then add your own flair.

Stitch in the ditch

This is where you quilt in the line of the seam, so it doesn't show up on the quilt. Since this method does not add to the design element of the quilt, I don't recommend it. Though it can be useful to add stability to a quilt before you do other quilting. It is usually stitched using a walking foot with the feed dogs up.

Straight-line quilting

It is best to use a walking foot for straight-line quilting. Try spacing your lines at different intervals and at different angles to add more interest to your quilt. A Hera marker or masking (painter's) tape can be used to mark your quilting guidelines.

Outline quilting

If you are looking for a way to outline blocks, try stitching ¼in on either side of the seam. This will give a crisp look and allow your quilting to shine. The quilting in Star Flower Table Topper includes an example of this. It is usually stitched using a walking foot with the feed dogs up.

Free-motion quilting

This method is done by lowering the feed dogs and using the darning foot. You are in control of the design and the stitch length. It takes practice, but once you master the technique it opens up endless possibilities in your quilting designs – essentially, it is like drawing with your machine. If you are a beginner, you may wish to test it out on a few spare quilt sandwich squares or a small project before tackling a large quilt. I used a version of free-motion quilting on all of the smaller quilts in this book.

Gentle curving lines

Allowing the quilted lines to ebb and flow will give a softer, more flowing feel. You can use a walking foot with the feed dogs up, or put the feed dogs down and use the darning foot instead. Where possible, I use the seams of my rows as guidelines so that my lines don't slowly get wider at one end of the quilt, which would result in more quilting on one side of the quilt compared to the other. Under the Sea features some quilting of this style.

Highlight the piecing

With this method of quilting, different motifs are placed in the quilting blocks and pieces to set them off. Remembering Ida is an example of this kind of quilting.

Overall design

This is where the same design is stitched over the whole quilt surface to showcase the quilt as a whole, rather than highlight individual elements. Zoodles and the background of Star Flower Table Topper are examples of this style of quilting.

Fit the theme

Here, the theme or inspiration for the quilt is taken through into the quilting, like the bubbles in Beaded Curtain to make them look like lava lamps, or the swirling starfish-like patterns in Blowin' in the Wind.

SQUARING-UP YOUR QUILT

This step is in preparation for binding your quilt. Start by placing a 6 x 24in ruler in one corner of your quilt, so that the 6in side is along the bottom edge and the 24in side runs up the side edge.

Straighten and adjust your quilt top edge so that it lines up along your ruler and you have a 90-degree angle at the corner. Trim the excess backing and wadding (batting). Continue around the edge of your quilt creating straight edges and 90-degree angles at the corners.

BINDING

The binding gives a finished edge to your quilted quilt. It is like a frame and is the last design choice you will make on your quilt. Audition different bindings by placing fabric along the quilt's edge so that only ¼in is showing. This will give you a feel for what your binding will look like on your quilt.

Binding can be cut on the straight grain of your fabric or on the bias (at a 45-degree angle). A straight-grain binding is faster and requires less fabric. A bias-cut binding will wear better. Whatever your chosen method, cut enough 2½in wide strips so that when joined with 45-degree seams the long strip will go all around your quilt plus 8–10in.

1 Right sides together, sew your binding strips into one long length using 45-degree seams. Press the seams open to reduce bulk and trim the 'ears'.

2 Fold the strip in half lengthwise, wrong sides together, and press.

3 Working from the right side and starting part way down one edge – I usually start on the bottom edge – match the raw edges of the binding to the raw edges of the quilt, leaving an 8–10in tail.

4 Sew in place. When you come to a corner, pull your binding back so it lines up with the next edge of your quilt. Finger press and carefully bring the end of the binding back so it lines up with the next edge of your quilt. Pin the resulting pleat at the corner. Then start sewing down the next edge. This is called a mitred corner.

5 When you get about 15in from where you began sewing your binding, stop. Line up your two binding ends along the edge of your quilt, folding back where they meet and creating a ½in gap between them. From each fold, measure back 1¹⁄₈in and cut the end of your binding. Take the left side of the binding and line up the edge that is next to the quilt to right side of the binding that is away from the quilt – the short side of each will run down the long side of the other. Pin and sew a 45-degree seam. Trim the seam allowance and continue to sew the binding in place.

TIP When joining the ends of my binding, I always check to make sure everything fits before I trim the seam allowance.

6 Fold the binding over to the back of the quilt and neatly slipstitch the folded edge to the backing fabric by hand.

QUILT LABELS

It is a good idea to add a label to your quilt. It should contain the name of the quilt, who made it, where they live, the date it was finished and any other information you would like to include. I find the easiest way for me to add a label is to fold an 8in square of fabric in half along the diagonal.

Using a permanent fabric pen, I write the information I wish to include onto one half of the folded square triangle. Then I sew the raw edges of the triangle into a corner on the back of the quilt when sewing the binding in place. Then all I have to do is hand slipstitch the folded diagonal edge of the label to the quilt backing.

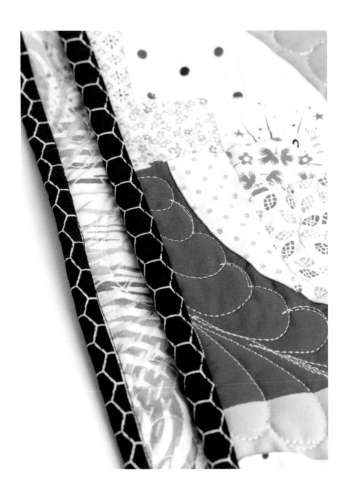

TEMPLATES

Templates are shown at actual size. Downloadable versions of these templates are available at www.davidandcharles.com.

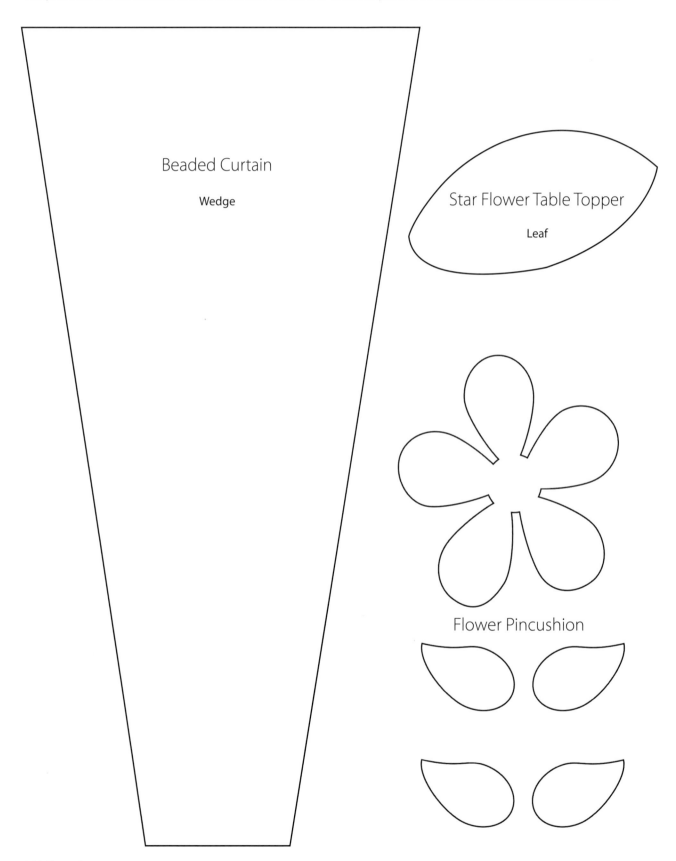

Beaded Curtain

Wedge

Star Flower Table Topper

Leaf

Flower Pincushion

Mary's Garden

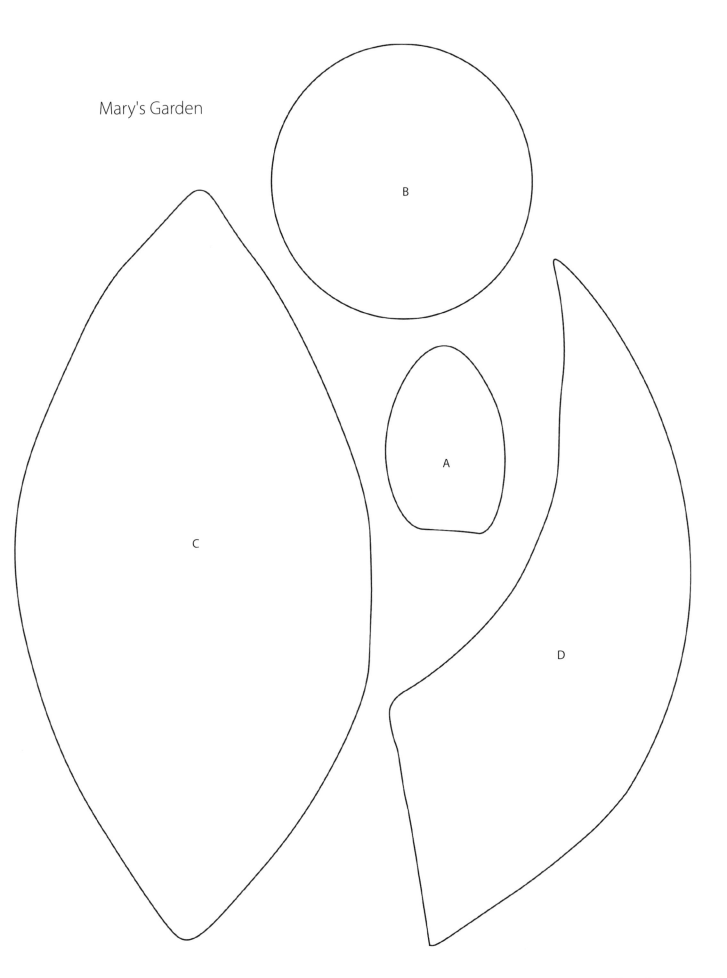

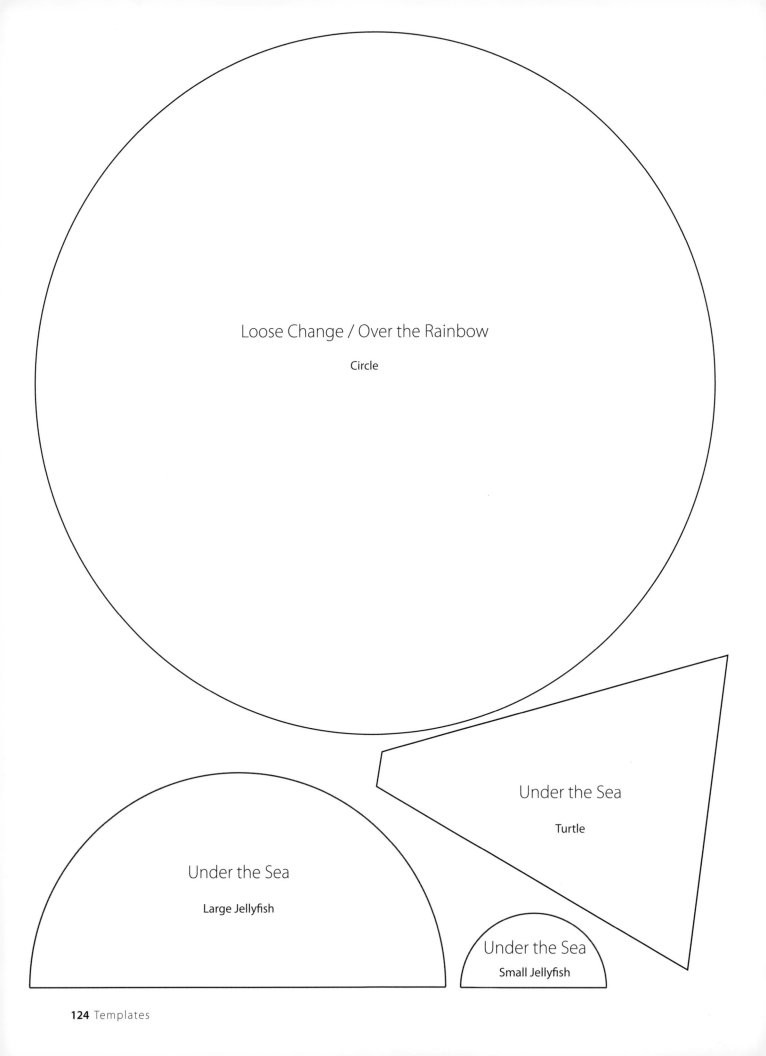

Loose Change / Over the Rainbow

Circle

Under the Sea

Turtle

Under the Sea

Large Jellyfish

Under the Sea

Small Jellyfish

Blowin' in the Wind

Leaves

ABOUT THE AUTHOR

Emily Bailey is a quilter, designer and teacher who is passionate about making one-of-a-kind modern scrappy quilts. Growing up in a family of artists and makers, she was always encouraged to create and develop her talents. She thought she would be a fashion designer, but after the birth of her three sons discovered that quilting was more her style. Emily loves being a part of the quilting community, and knows wherever she goes to teach and mingle with other quilters she will have instant friends.

Emily has been designing quilts for twenty years, with a focus on fun and easy-to-understand patterns. Her work has been published in *Love of Quilting*, *McCall's Quilting* and *Simply Quilts*. She teaches through her website, YouTube and at live events.

www.auntemsquilts.com

ACKNOWLEDGEMENTS

Thank you to my family. My parents who taught me to develop my talents and were such examples of doing just that. My hubby who puts up with all the creative clutter I create along with my quilts. My children for cheering me on. My sister, Becky Reed, for all the beautiful photos she takes of my quilts and quilting processes. Thank you to my dear friend and retreat roommate, Ruth Davis, for quilting all the large quilts in this book. Her quilting skills astonish me. Victoria Findlay Wolf who taught me this method and encouraged me to take it further. Thank you to Sarah Callard for giving me this opportunity and for helping me to navigate the process. Thank you to Anne Williams, her editing skills are amazing. And a big thank you to everyone at David & Charles for making this such an incredible book. I am in awe!

INDEX